Contents

KU-590-614

The Fill Tool   109

The Artistic Media Tool   135

The Interactive Tools   139

First steps

This chapter gets you started with CorelDRAW quickly. It shows you how to launch CorelDRAW and create new (or open existing) documents at the same time, then save them to disk. You'll learn how to specify which toolbars and docker windows display, and how to work with different document views and zoom levels (including saving/opening views with View Manager). You'll also enhance your use of CorelDRAW with Document Info and the Property Bar. Finally, you'll save your settings as workspaces, then connect to a design-orientated Web site for tips and general assistance.

Covers

Chapter One

Starting CorelDRAW

To launch CorelDRAW, click the Start button on the Task Bar at the base of the Windows screen. Then click Programs. In the Program menu, click CorelDRAW 9. In the sub-menu, select CorelDRAW 9.

A special screen launches. Perform step 1 OR 2:

To open existing files after you've started CorelDRAW, press Ctrl+O. The Open Drawing dialog launches – follow step 3 below.

Before you carry out step 3, do the following:

- **use the Look in: field to locate the drive which hosts the file you want to open**
- **(if necessary) double-click one or more folders till you locate the relevant file**

If you want to see what a file looks like *before* opening it, ensure the Preview box is ticked.

1 Click here to create a blank file

2 Click here to open an existing file

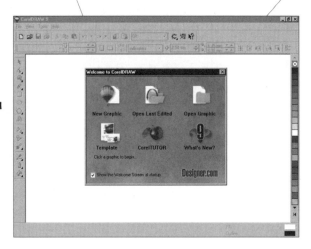

If you performed step 2, do the following:

3 Double-click the file you want to open

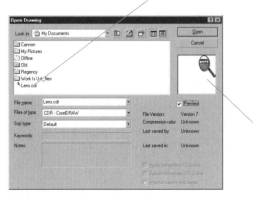

Preview window

The CorelDRAW screen

 The other screen elements are common to most or all Windows programs. (See your Windows documentation for how to use them.)

 To save previously unsaved documents, press Ctrl+S. In the Save Drawing dialog, use the Save in: field to select a host drive. Double-click one or more folders, as necessary. Finally, name the document in the File name: box, then click Save. (To save files which have been saved before simply press Ctrl+S.)

 The commands available in the Property Bar vary according to which object is selected – see page 14.

Whether you create a new CorelDRAW document or open an existing one, the result will look like this:

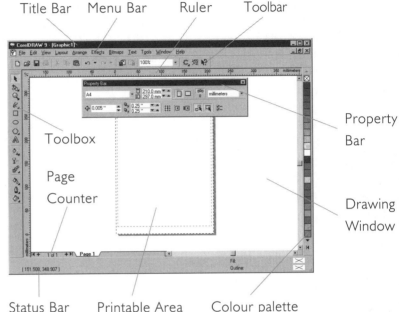

Title Bar   Menu Bar   Ruler   Toolbar

Toolbox

Page Counter

Property Bar

Drawing Window

Status Bar   Printable Area   Colour palette

The following are details of CorelDRAW-specific screen components:

Toolbars
Toolbars are collections of icons. By clicking an appropriate icon, you can launch a specific feature. This saves you having to pull down menus. CorelDRAW provides a variety of toolbars.

Drawing Window & Printable Area
You can work anywhere in the Drawing Window, but only the objects placed on the Printable Area can be printed.

Property Bar
The Property Bar is a special on-screen toolbar which displays commands in a convenient and easily accessible format.

When you're on the first page of a document, the Page Back arrow changes to a "+": click on it to insert a new page at the beginning of the active document. The same thing happens to the Page Forward arrow when you're on the last page of a document.

Page Counter

CorelDRAW lets you create multi-page documents. The Page Counter displays the total number of pages in a document, and tells you which page is currently active. You can also use the Page Counter to move from page to page very easily: simply click the relevant page tab, or click the Page Forward or Page Back arrows.

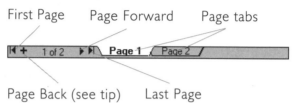

First Page   Page Forward   Page tabs

Page Back (see tip)   Last Page

Colour palette

You use colour palettes to apply colours to object fills.

Flyouts provide access to tool variations. For example, the Zoom Tool flyout:

shows two incarnations:

 Zoom Tool

 Pan Tool

(For more on flyouts and the Pan Tool, see the facing page.)

Toolbox

The Toolbox provides access to an assortment of special tools. By clicking the appropriate icon (and occasionally by selecting from a subsidiary flyout, too), you launch the relevant tool. Tools are discussed as they occur.

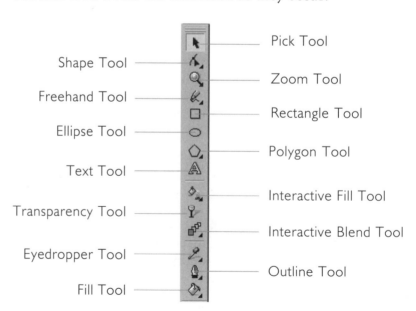

Pick Tool

Shape Tool

Zoom Tool

Freehand Tool

Rectangle Tool

Ellipse Tool

Polygon Tool

Text Tool

Interactive Fill Tool

Transparency Tool

Interactive Blend Tool

Eyedropper Tool

Outline Tool

Fill Tool

Document Info

To launch tool flyouts (see the facing page), do the following:

Click the arrow

The Pan Tool (see the facing page) moves drawings within the current window without changing the Zoom level.

After clicking the Pan Tool icon, move the mouse pointer (a hand) over the active drawing. Click and hold down the left mouse button, then drag the drawing to a new location. Finally, release the mouse button.

CorelDRAW documents can quickly become complex. To help you find your way around them, you can use a feature called Document Info. Document Info lists document components, under the following headings:

File	Filename/address details
Document	Document statistics (e.g. page count, paper size)
Graphic Objects	Details of graphic objects (e.g. lines)
Text Statistics	Text information (e.g. paragraph/word counts and fonts used)
Bitmaps	Details of included bitmaps
Styles	Details of styles used
Effects	Details of effects
Fills	Details of fills and colours used
Outlines	Details of outlines used

Using Document Info

Pull down the File menu and click Document Info. Now do the following:

2 View the document statistics

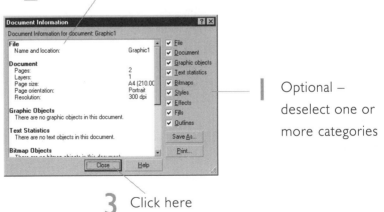

Optional – deselect one or more categories

3 Click here

Using templates

To create a new blank document after you've started CorelDRAW (see page 8 for how to do it at start-up), click New in step 1, instead, then ignore steps 2–3.
(Alternatively, ignore steps 1–3 and simply press Ctrl+N.)

Templates are collections of formatting and drawings. Their advantage is that they save you time and effort. When you create a new file based on a template, you automatically have access to all the associated formatting and drawings.

Creating a new document based on a template
Pull down the File menu and do the following:

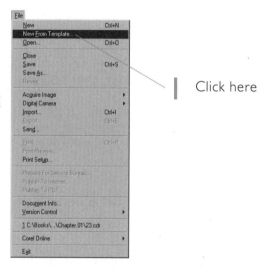

Click here

You can also opt to create a new document based on a template when you're in the process of starting CorelDRAW.
In the launch screen, click this icon:

Now follow steps 2–4 here.

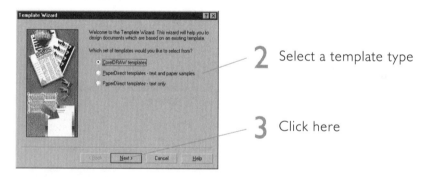

2 Select a template type

3 Click here

4 Complete the additional dialogs which launch, following the on-screen instructions

Working with toolbars

You can also use a shortcut to display (or hide) a toolbar. In the menu which launches, select a toolbar entry.

Re step 1 – to ensure a toolbar appears on-screen, do the following:

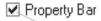

Click here (a tick appears)

(To hide a toolbar, repeat the above – the tick vanishes.)

To move a toolbar, click in its border during on-screen editing and drag it to a new location.

In both 'Adding icons' and 'Removing icons', perform step 2 when you've finished.

You can select which toolbars display. You can also copy or remove icons, and reposition toolbars on the screen.

Displaying/hiding Toolbars

Right-click any toolbar. In the menu, select Toolbars. Now do the following:

Click the toolbar(s) you want to display or hide – see the DON'T FORGET tip

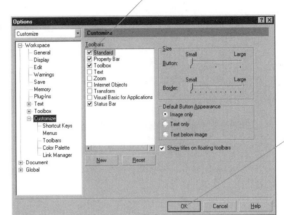

2 Click here

Adding icons

To add a new icon to an on-screen toolbar, click Toolbars in the Customize list on the left of the above dialog – the dialog changes. In the Commands: section, double-click a command category (prefixed by ⊞) then select a sub-category. Icons now display on the right of the dialog – hold the mouse pointer over each to view a definition e.g:

Zoom To All Objects
F4

Drag the appropriate icon to the relevant on-screen toolbar.

Removing icons

To delete an icon from an on-screen toolbar, click Toolbars in the Customize list on the left of the Options dialog. Drag any icon off an on-screen toolbar (anywhere except onto a toolbar). Release the mouse button to remove the icon.

Using the Property Bar

The Property Bars shown as examples here have been 'resized' – see below.

The Property Bar displays commands on-screen. It does so in a format which is immediately accessible, and – even more usefully – it only displays commands which relate to the currently selected object. This means that the Property Bar can have incarnations which change quite dramatically:

If (when an object is selected and the Property Bar is on-screen) you click a tool in the Toolbox, CorelDRAW updates the commands in the Property Bar accordingly.

Property Bar when text is selected

Property Bar when a polygon is selected

Property Bar when no object is selected – i.e. it displays Page Setup commands

If no toolbar is currently on-screen, you can use another method to launch or hide the Property Bar.

Pull down the Window menu and click Toolbars. In the Toolbars section on the right of the Options dialog, select or deselect Property Bar. Click OK.

Launching the Property Bar

If the Property Bar isn't already visible, right-click any toolbar. In the menu, select Property Bar.

(Repeat this to hide the Property Bar).

Closing the Property Bar

Click the Close button – ⊠ – in the upper right-hand corner of the Property Bar.

Customising the Property Bar

The Property Bar acts like a toolbar. This means you can:

* position it on the top, bottom, left or right of the screen (this is called 'docking'). To do this, drag the Property Bar's Title bar to the correct location

* resize it, using normal Windows techniques

Working with docker windows

To 'undock' a docker window (i.e. position it elsewhere on-screen), simply drag its Title bar to the relevant location.

(Double-click the Title bar to return the window to the docked position.)

To close a docker window, click this button:

in the top right-hand corner.

When collapsed, docker windows look like this:

Many CorelDRAW features (e.g. View Manager – see page 20) are available from docker windows. These are dedicated dialog boxes which (by default) are 'docked' on the right of the screen, for ease of access.

Launching docker windows
Pull down the Window menu and click Dockers. In the sub-menu, select the appropriate docker.

Shrinking docker windows
To collapse a docker, carry out step 1 below:

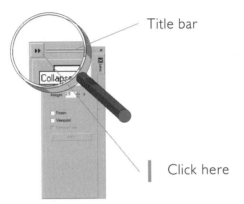

Title bar

Click here

Expanding docker windows
Carry out step 1 below:

Click here

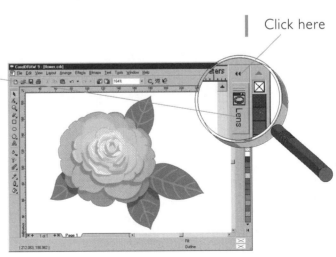

Using Undo and Redo

A very useful feature in CorelDRAW is the ability to reverse editing actions. Most changes can be undone (however, you can't undo changes in zoom levels).

CorelDRAW lets you specify the number of consecutive undos you can carry out (you can have as many as your computer's memory permits). You can also perform multiple undos.

To undo more than one action, do the following in the Standard toolbar:

Click here

In the list, select multiple undos (if you choose an item lower down the list, all earlier items are automatically selected).

To perform multiple redos, follow the actions in the HOT TIP – but instead refer to this icon in the Standard toolbar:

Undoing the last action
Press Ctrl+Z, or Alt+Backspace.

Setting Undo levels
By default, CorelDRAW allocates 99 undo levels. If you want more (or fewer), pull down the Tools menu and choose Options. Then follow the procedures below.

1 Click Workspace, then General

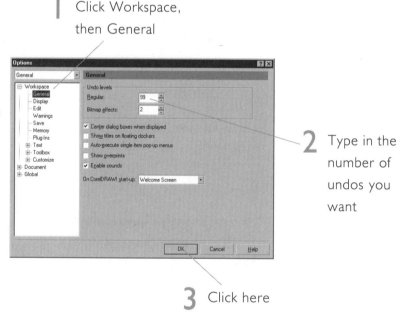

2 Type in the number of undos you want

3 Click here

Redoing the last action
You can even undo the last undo – CorelDRAW calls this 'redoing'. Simply press Ctrl+Shift+Z.

Using views

CorelDRAW lets you work with documents in various 'views'. These are specialised ways of looking at your work.

Full Screen Preview displays drawings in Enhanced view (see page 18).

Full Screen Preview

Sometimes, it's useful to view your work without any of the screen components we discussed on pages 9 and 10 being visible. Use Full Screen Preview to achieve this. Full Screen Preview provides a clearer idea of what your drawing will look like when printed.

To preview your work, press F9.

To some extent, the effect of imposing views depends on the number of colours your display is currently using.

A CorelDRAW graphic in Full Screen Preview

These views only affect the way CorelDRAW objects display on-screen; they have no effect on image content.

To return to your normal view, press F9 again. Alternatively, press Esc or the Spacebar.

Simple Wireframe view

This view hides just about all complex object properties (including fills, extrusions, and intermediate blend shapes), and bitmaps display in black-and-white. Simple Wireframe view displays only the outlines of objects. This can make editing your drawings a lot easier and quicker, especially if they're complex.

To enter Simple Wireframe view, pull down the View menu and click Simple Wireframe.

Wireframe view

This view is somewhat less Draconian than Simple Wireframe. Fills and outlines do not display; instead, drawings are shown in 'skeleton' form, but with rather more detail. Like Simple Wireframe, Wireframe view can make editing your drawings a lot quicker.

These views only affect the way CorelDRAW objects display on-screen; they have no effect on image content.

To enter Wireframe view, pull down the View menu and click Wireframe.

The image from page 17 in Wireframe view

Draft view

This view displays solid fills and low-resolution bitmaps accurately. Fountain fills, however, are represented by solid colours (based on the first and last fill colours) and other fills (e.g. 2-colour fills) with specific patterns.

To enter Draft view, click Draft in the View menu.

PostScript is a detailed page description (programming) language used to print to laser printers and other high-resolution printing devices.

Normal view

This view displays all fills accurately (with the exception of PostScript fills).

To enter Normal view, pull down the View menu and click Normal.

Enhanced view

This view maximises view properties to provide the best possible display. In addition, PostScript fills display accurately.

To enter Enhanced view, pull down the View menu and click Enhanced.

Using Zoom

To close the Zoom toolbar, click the Close button:

in the upper right hand corner.

You can also use the Property Bar to set zoom levels.

First, ensure it's on-screen (for how to do this, see page 14). Then click the Zoom Tool:

in the Toolbox. The Property Bar is now configured for Zoom:

Carry out any of steps 1–5.

If the Toolbox Zoom Tool is active, left-click to zoom in or right-click to zoom out.

Often, it's important to be able to view sections of your drawings in close up ('zoom in'). On other occasions, you'll want to take an overview ('zoom out'). CorelDRAW lets you do both very easily.

First, make sure the Zoom toolbar is visible (if it isn't, right-click any toolbar and select Zoom):

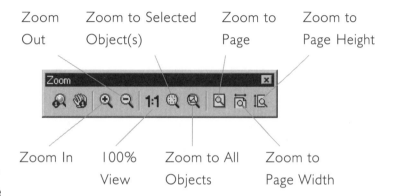

Zoom Out   Zoom to Selected Object(s)   Zoom to Page   Zoom to Page Height

Zoom In   100% View   Zoom to All Objects   Zoom to Page Width

Using the Zoom toolbar

Perform any of the following, as required:

1 To zoom in or out, click the Zoom In or Zoom Out button respectively (repeat as often as necessary).

2 To view your drawing at the dimensions it will have when printed, click the 100% View button.

3 Click Zoom to Selected Objects to have those objects which have been selected fill the screen, or Zoom to All Objects to view all objects (whether selected or not).

4 To view all of the printable page, click Zoom to Page.

5 To view the document widthways, click Zoom to Page Width. Or click Zoom to Page Height to view it lengthways.

Using View Manager

Use View Manager to move around quickly and easily in especially complex or multi-page documents.

View Manager is a specialist adaptation of CorelDRAW's Zoom feature. It lets you allocate names to specific views of an open document. Once you've named a view, you can return to it very easily.

Creating a view

First zoom in on the object(s) you want to save as a view. Press Ctrl+F2. Then carry out the following actions:

Re step 2 – to enter your own view name, do the following:

`View Nev P 1    181%`

Click the Name section; in the revised box, type in the new name

Click here

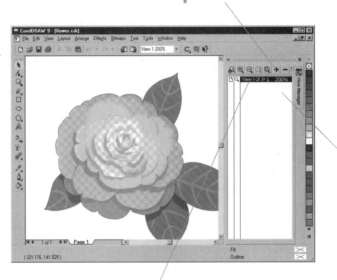

The View Manager docker

Repeat steps 1–3 for as many views as you want to create.

2 Optional – delete the standard view name and type in your own (see the HOT TIP)

3 Press Enter

To close the View Manager, click the Close button:

in the upper right hand corner.

Jumping to a view

To jump straight to a view, do the following:

`Miniature  P 1    91%`

Double-click the relevant view entry (but not the Name section)

Using workspaces

You can:

- customise many aspects of the way you use CorelDRAW

- save the customisation details as a 'workspace'

- apply the workspace/customisation details with a few mouse clicks

In this way you can, in effect, create and apply different versions of CorelDRAW, with settings specific to given purposes or situations.

We've already seen (on page 16) how to customise one aspect of the way you use CorelDRAW; other aspects you can customise include:

- the way CorelDRAW's display operates

- the way CorelDRAW handles text

- the way CorelDRAW handles internal memory

Memory settings should only be changed with caution.

Creating a workspace

Pull down the Tools menu and carry out the following actions:

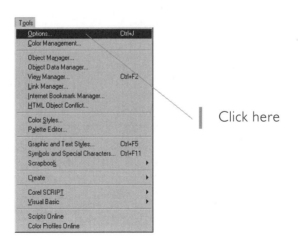

Click here

Now perform the following steps (but see the HOT TIP on the left):

Before you carry out step 2, select a program area in the Workspace drop-down list:

Workspace list

2 Ensure Workspace is selected

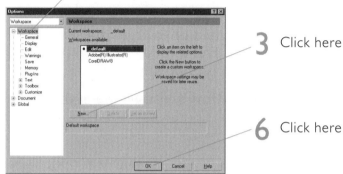

3 Click here

6 Click here

Now complete the dialog on the right of the list. Repeat as often as necessary. Finally, perform steps 2–6 on the right.

4 Name the new workspace

If the Workspace list (see the above tip) isn't visible, do the following:

Click here

5 Click here

Applying a workspace

Follow step 1 on page 21, and step 2 above. In the Workspaces available: field in the Options dialog, highlight the workspace you want to apply. Click this button:

Now carry out step 6 above.

Corel Online

 To access the Links site, follow steps 1–2. In step 3 on page 24, however, click Links. Click an overall link category e.g: Design Inspirations
Follow the on-screen instructions.

 The Corel Online Welcome page also has helpful articles. Follow steps 1–2. Now click a topic e.g: Setting Your CorelDRAW® Defaults

 Many other menus also contain useful Web links. For example, the Fonts Online entry in the Text menu takes you to a site which supplies articles about typography.

CorelDRAW has inbuilt links to dedicated, design-related World Wide Web pages. Provided you have:

- a modem

- a live connection to an Internet service provider

you can connect almost immediately to:

- helpful articles which are specific to CorelDRAW-related questions and topics

- dedicated newsgroups

- a special Links site which provides useful links to other design-related Web sites, to help you improve your use of CorelDRAW

- a special site from which you can download software updates

Launching Corel Online

With a live Internet connection, pull down the File menu and do the following:

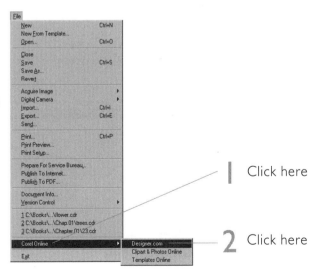

1 Click here

2 Click here

To access a newsgroup, click Interact in step 3. Click newsgroups, then select a newsgroup e.g:

Software Forum

Follow the on-screen instructions.

To download software updates, do the following:

In step 3, click Freebies. Now do the following:

Click a topic

Read the on-screen instructions. When you're ready to download, click:

Click here to download

The sites described here are liable to change over time.

The Corel Welcome page launches. Carry out steps 3–4:

3 Click Focus

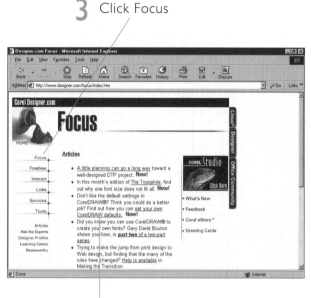

4 Click any article

The end result:

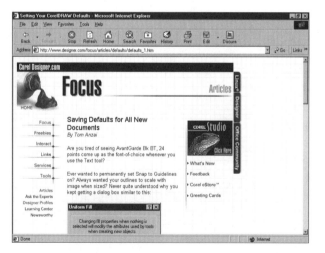

One of the many available articles

Basic drawing

In this chapter, you'll learn how to select CorelDRAW objects. Then you'll create simple shapes (lines, curves, ellipses, circles, rectangles and squares). Finally, you'll also learn about shortcuts which allow you to align the objects you create, easily and conveniently.

Covers

Chapter Two

Selection techniques

CorelDRAW makes use of standard Windows selection procedures. For instance, with the Pick tool in the Toolbox activated, clicking on a drawing object's outline 'selects' it (this means that any editing actions you undertake apply solely to this object). However, there are other selection routes which are more or less specific to CorelDRAW.

Using marquees

This is a very useful technique for selecting one or more objects at a time. Make sure the Pick tool is activated. Then simply move the mouse pointer to one corner of the (imaginary) rectangle which contains the object(s) you want to select. Click and hold down the left mouse button as you drag out a dashed rectangle that completely surrounds the objects. When you release the button, all the enclosed objects are selected.

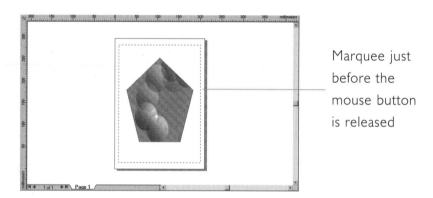

Marquee just before the mouse button is released

Using Shift

Another way to select several objects is to activate the Pick tool and hold down one Shift key as you click sequentially on the object outlines.

Selecting all objects automatically

You can have CorelDRAW select all objects on the current page within the active document. To do this, double-click the Pick tool.

Working with selected objects

When you select an object in CorelDRAW, it's surrounded with eight green handles:

If you hold down one Ctrl key as you resize or stretch an object, changes are made in 100% increments.

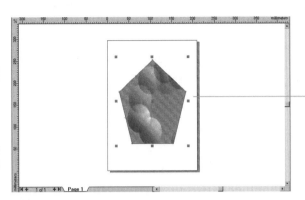

After the mouse button has been released; the object is selected

If you hold down one Shift key as you resize or stretch an object, changes are made from the centre outwards.

You can perform a variety of operations on selected objects. These include:

*   moving/resizing

*   reshaping/rotation

*   filling

*   customising outlines

If you hold down the Spacebar as you move an object around the screen, copies of the object are left behind – this is a useful copying technique which is specific to CorelDRAW.

You move CorelDRAW objects with more or less standard Windows techniques. The same applies to resizing (i.e. dragging a centre handle stretches objects, thus disrupting their height/width ratio, while dragging on a corner handle resizes them proportionally). We'll be looking at the use of outlines, reshaping/rotation and fills in later chapters.

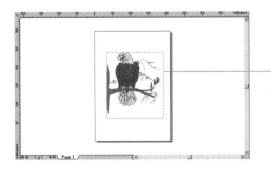

A graphical object in the course of being resized – note the dashed box

Object locking

When you've created complex documents in CorelDRAW (i.e. documents with numerous object components and/or objects which are themselves complex), it can sometimes happen that objects which you don't wish moved or resized can be affected inadvertently. To prevent this, you can opt to 'lock' specific objects to the underlying drawing area. Locked objects cannot be:

Nearly all objects can be locked – the main exceptions are:
- **blended or extruded objects**
- **objects with drop shadows**

- moved or resized

- filled

- deleted

Locking one or more objects

Use the techniques discussed on page 26 to select one or more objects. Pull down the Arrange menu and do the following:

To unlock one or more locked objects, first select them. Then pull down the Arrange menu and click Unlock Object or Unlock All Objects, as appropriate.

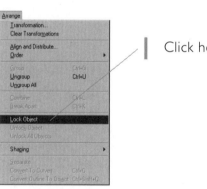

Click here

A locked object – notice the transformed handles

Digger selection

Another feature of complex documents in CorelDRAW is the difficulty in finding specific objects which are hidden under others. There is, however, a way round this: digger selection

Look at the next illustration:

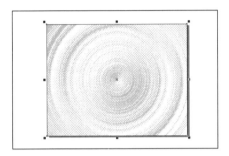

Here, a large textured object sits on top of another, smaller object (currently unseen). The visible object has been selected; the problem is how to select the lower object. In this instance, it would be simple enough merely to drag the large object to one side. However, if there were numerous objects, the problem would be more difficult. The answer is to use digger selection.

Using digger selection

This is the hidden object's centre X icon:

Hold down the Alt key while you click varying locations on the uppermost object. Eventually, this is the result:

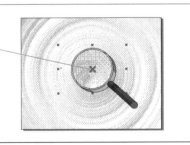

The hidden object's selection handles appear

Move the mouse pointer over the centre X and drag the hidden object out.

Working with lines

Many drawing operations are undertaken with the help of the Freehand or Bezier tools. These are accessible from within the Toolbox. Follow step 1 below, then 2 OR 3:

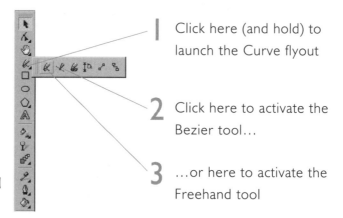

1 Click here (and hold) to launch the Curve flyout

2 Click here to activate the Bezier tool...

3 ...or here to activate the Freehand tool

If you hold down the Ctrl key as you define lines with the Freehand tool, they're constrained to 15 degree increments.

Using the Freehand tool

The Freehand cursor is a cross with a wavy line. Click in your drawing where you want the line to start. Then click where you want it to end. If you want the line to continue, click one line-end and draw another segment. Repeat this as often as necessary.

Using the Bezier tool

The Bezier cursor is a cross with a *circled* wavy line. Click where you want the line to start. Then click where you want it to finish. If you want the line to continue, click where you want the next line to end. Repeat this as often as necessary. Press the Spacebar twice when you've finished (or activate another tool by clicking it in the Toolbox).

If you define additional segments, click as close to the line-end as possible.

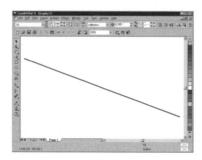

A Bezier line

Working with freehand curves

To control how close the curve is to the originating mouse movement, refer to the Property Bar and do the following:

Type in a smoothness setting

(The higher the setting, the less accurate the effect.)

You can easily erase part of a freehand curve *before* you carry out step 4. Simply hold down one Shift key while you drag backwards over your curve. Release Shift to resume drawing.

If you define additional curves, click as close to the endpoint as possible.

Drawing freehand curves

Drawing freehand curves is one of CorelDRAW's least user-friendly operations, in the sense that using it effectively requires some artistic ability. In fact, it's probably the feature you'll use least of all. However, freehand drawing in CorelDRAW can create highly original effects. Think of it like using a pencil, or an Etch-a-Sketch.

To draw curves with the Freehand tool, launch the Curve flyout (see page 30 for how to do this). Then select the Freehand tool. Perform the following operations:

1 Place the mouse pointer where you want your curve to start

2 Hold down the left mouse button

3 Drag out the curves you need

4 Release the mouse button when you've finished

Joining curves

If you want to create a new curve and join it to an existing one, place the mouse pointer over the endpoint of the original. Then follow steps 2 to 4 above.

The end result:

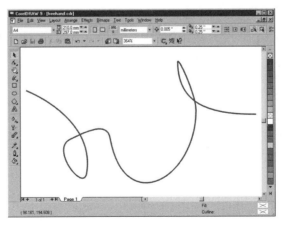

A sample curve

Working with ellipses

CorelDRAW makes creating ellipses easy.

 To create a circle, carry out steps 1–2. Before you perform step 3, however, hold down one Ctrl key. Now carry out step 4. Finally, release the Ctrl button.

Drawing an ellipse

In the Toolbox, do the following:

Click the Ellipse tool

 You can create an ellipse or circle from the centre outwards. Simply hold down one Shift key as you carry out the relevant procedures.

Now carry out these steps:

2 Place the mouse pointer where you want one corner of the ellipse to begin

3 Click and hold down the left mouse button

4 Drag to create the ellipse, then release the mouse button

The end result:

 To create a rectangle which fills the page, simply double-click the Rectangle Tool.

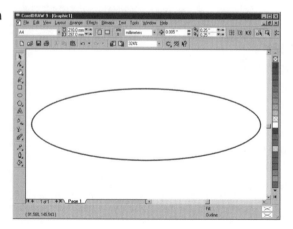

A sample ellipse

Working with rectangles

To create a square, carry out steps 1-2. Before you perform step 3, however, hold down one Ctrl key. Now carry out step 4. Finally, release the Ctrl button.

You can easily create rectangles in CorelDRAW.

Drawing a rectangle

In the Toolbox, do the following:

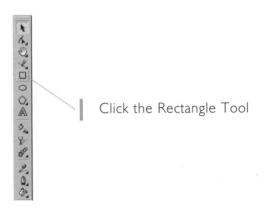

Click the Rectangle Tool

You can create a rectangle or square from the centre outwards. Simply hold down one Shift key as you carry out the relevant procedures.

Now carry out these steps:

2 Place the mouse pointer where you want one corner of the rectangle to begin

3 Click and hold down the left mouse button

4 Drag to create the rectangle, then release the mouse button

To round a rectangle corner, ensure the Rectangle tool is active. Now click the corner. Move the mouse pointer away from the corner, then back; it changes to a black arrow. Drag the corner inwards to round it.

The end result:

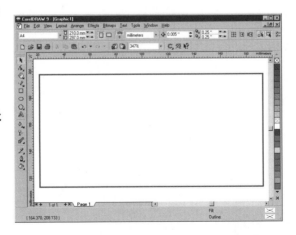

A sample rectangle

Using grids

CorelDRAW provides several aids which allow you to align objects automatically and precisely (this is also useful when you resize objects). One of the foremost of these aids is grids.

Grids consist of a uniform arrangement of points to which objects can be 'snapped' i.e. aligned automatically.

Re step 1 – Grid is a sub-category of the Document list. If the Document list isn't visible, do the following:

Click here

Setting up a grid

Press Ctrl+J. Then carry out the following steps:

1 Click Grid

2 Activate Frequency

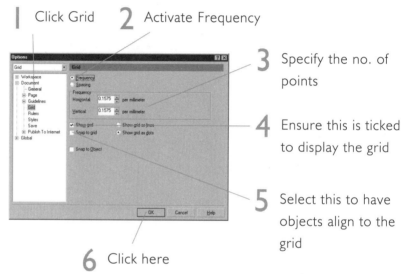

3 Specify the no. of points

4 Ensure this is ticked to display the grid

5 Select this to have objects align to the grid

6 Click here

By default, grids display as lines (designed specifically to resemble graph paper, for ease of use). If, however, you want to display them as dots (where each dot represents the intersection of two lines), select Show grid as dots before you carry out step 6.

The grid in action:

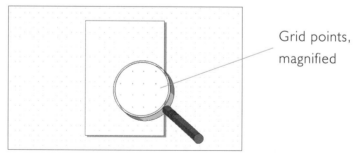

Grid points, magnified

Using rulers

You can move rulers onto the page.
Place the mouse pointer over a ruler. Hold down Shift; left-click and drag the ruler to a new location.
(To return it to its original location, hold down Shift and double-click the ruler.)

Rulers are another aid to aligning objects. Both horizontal and vertical rulers are flexible, on-screen calibrations which you can use to size and position drawing components.

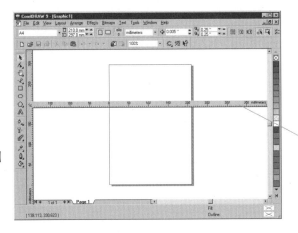

Repositioned ruler – see the HOT TIP

To hide rulers, repeat the procedure described under 'Displaying rulers'.

Displaying rulers

If the rulers aren't currently displaying, pull down the View menu and choose Rulers.

Specifying ruler settings

Double-click a ruler. Now perform the following steps:

Optional – click here, then select a new unit (e.g. inches) in the list

You can also display the ruler by activating Show Rulers here:
(To hide the ruler, ensure the tick disappears.)

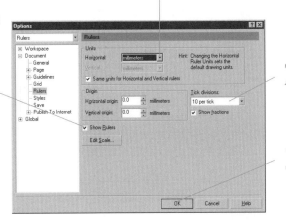

2 Complete these fields, as appropriate

3 Click here

Using guidelines

To have objects align to guidelines, make sure Snap To Guidelines is activated in the View menu.

Whereas grids can be used to position all the objects within a particular drawing, you use guidelines to position *individual* objects. Guidelines are movable, non-printing lines on screen which are saved with the host file. You can create as many guidelines as you need.

Creating standard guidelines

Guidelines are objects. This means they can be selected in the normal way. (Selected guidelines are red, unselected ones blue.)

1 Place the mouse pointer over the Horizontal or Vertical ruler, as appropriate

2 Click and hold down the left mouse button

3 Drag a guideline onto the page

4 Release the mouse button

Guidelines in action:

To print guidelines, pull down the Tools menu and click Object Manager. In the Object Manager docker, do the following:

Click here

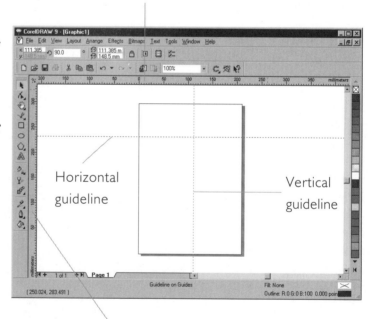

Horizontal ruler

Horizontal guideline

Vertical guideline

Vertical ruler

The flagged icon now looks like this:

...cont'd

Re step 1 – don't double-click.

To change the colour of a guideline, select it. Now drag a colour from the on-screen Colour Palette onto the guideline.
(See page 9 for details of screen components.)

You can apply preset guidelines. Select an existing guideline. In the Property Bar, click this icon:

In the dialog, select a preset (e.g. Basic Grid). Click OK.

To delete a slanting guideline, right-click it. In the menu, click Delete.

Creating slanting guidelines

A feature which is rare in other programs is the ability to define *sloping* guidelines. These are useful for positioning objects whose shape is non-standard.

To create a slanted guideline, first create a vertical or horizontal guideline (see page 36). Then do the following:

1 Place the mouse pointer over the guideline and click twice

2 Drag one of the 2 handles until the angle is correct

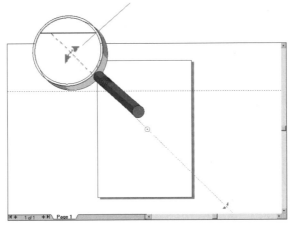

3 Release the mouse button

Moving guidelines

To reposition a guideline, move the mouse pointer over it. Click and hold down the left mouse button; drag the guideline to its new location. Release the mouse button to confirm the move.

Deleting horizontal/vertical guidelines

Place the mouse pointer over the guideline you want to remove. Click and hold down the left mouse button; drag the guideline back to the horizontal or vertical ruler. Release the mouse button to confirm the deletion.

Snapping to objects

 There is a snap hierarchy: Snap To Objects takes precedence over Snap To Grid or Snap To Guidelines.

There is one final technique you can use to align your drawings. When you create or reposition an object, you can have it snap automatically to (i.e. align with) another. This is possible because the various types of objects you work with in CorelDRAW (e.g. lines, curves, ellipses/circles, rectangles/squares, text, bitmaps) are allocated several convenient 'snap points' when created. These are usually located at the centre and perimeter.

Turning on Snap to Objects

To have objects you create or change snap to existing objects, pull down the View menu and click Snap To Objects.

Viewing snap points

To see an object's snap points, first make sure Snap to Objects is enabled. Then launch the Curve flyout (see page 30 for how to do this) and do the following:

Click here

 Activating the Snap To Objects feature has no effect on the alignment of *existing* objects.

2 Manoeuvre the mouse pointer over the object. CorelDRAW reveals snap points when the pointer encounters them:

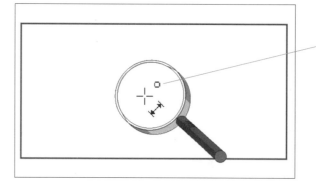

One snap point

Advanced drawing

This chapter shows you how to create complex Bezier curves and variable-sided polygons (pentagrams, stars, spirals and logarithmic spirals). We'll also discuss ways to manipulate objects, create specialised lines and work with nodes (which you can use to reshape lines/curves).

Covers

Chapter Three

Working with Bezier curves

In Chapter 2, we looked at how to create Bezier lines. CorelDRAW also lets you create Bezier curves. These are much more useful (and easier to draw) than freehand curves. When you create Bezier curves, you click to define the start and end points, then drag to define the extent of the curve; CorelDRAW does the rest.

Creating a Bezier curve

First, carry out the following actions:

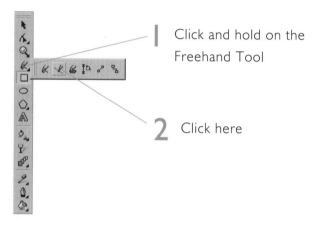

1 Click and hold on the Freehand Tool

2 Click here

3 Click where you want the curve to start, then hold down the mouse button and drag. Release the button

Control points

For how to use control points, see the DON'T FORGET tips on page 47.

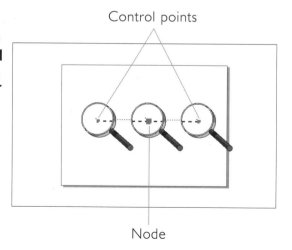

Node

CorelDRAW creates a central node and two control points.

...cont'd

Bear in mind the following:

- The depth of the curve is regulated by the distance between the control points and the node

 Holding down one Ctrl key as you define Bezier curves constrains them to 15° increments.

- The slope of the curve is regulated by the control point angle

4 Click where you want the curve to end, and drag to refine the curve. Release the mouse button

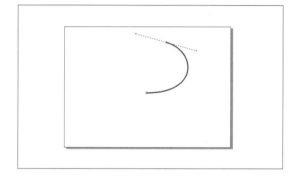

Here, one curve has been defined

5 Repeat step 4 if you want to create more curves

6 Press the Spacebar twice when you've finished defining the curve(s), or click another tool in the Toolbox

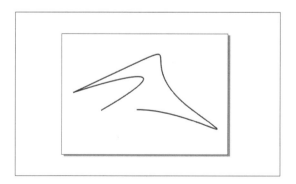

A completed series of curves

Working with polygons

CorelDRAW lets you create polygons quickly and very easily. By default, CorelDRAW creates 5-sided polygons; however, you can also specify how many sides the polygon should have. Additionally, you can create stars and spirals.

Holding down one Ctrl key as you define polygons, stars or spirals stops them from being stretched out of shape.

Holding down one Shift key as you define polygons, stars or spirals creates them from the centre outwards.

Creating a pentagon
Refer to the Toolbox. Carry out steps 1 and 3 below:

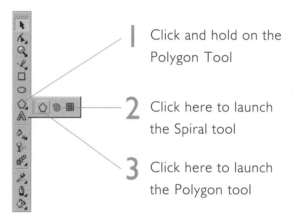

| Click and hold on the Polygon Tool

2 Click here to launch the Spiral tool

3 Click here to launch the Polygon tool

4 Click where you want one corner of the object to appear, then hold down the mouse button and drag to define it. Release the button

Creating a polygon with more or fewer than 5 sides
Follow steps 1 and 3 above. However, before you start to draw the polygon, double-click the Polygon tool in the Toolbox. Then do the following:

After B, follow step 4 above.

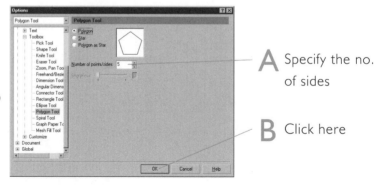

A Specify the no. of sides

B Click here

...cont'd

By default, spirals have 4 revolutions. **If you want more or fewer, double-click the Spiral tool:**

in the Toolbox *after* **you've carried out steps 1 and 2 on page 42. In the Options dialog, type a revised number in the Number of revolutions: field. Click OK. Now create the spiral.**

You can create logarithmic spirals **(spirals using dimensions which are proportional to the logarithms of numbers).** **Launch the Options dialog (see the tip above). Choose Logarithmic (and specify the no. of revolutions). Click OK. Finally, create the spiral in the normal way.**

Creating a star

Follow steps 1 and 3 on page 42. However, before you begin to create the star, double-click the Polygon tool in the Toolbox. Then do the following:

A Click Star or Polygon as Star

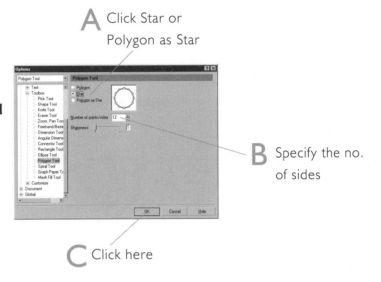

B Specify the no. of sides

C Click here

D Carry out step 4 on page 42

Creating a spiral

Carry out steps 1 and 2 on page 42 (however, if you want your spiral to have more or fewer than four revolutions, carry out the procedures described in the DON'T FORGET tip on the left before creating it). Now carry out the following steps:

3 Place the cursor where you want the spiral to start

4 Hold down the left mouse button, then drag to define the spiral

5 Release the mouse button

Manipulating objects

Once you've created drawing objects, CorelDRAW lets you amend them in a variety of ways. We've already discussed resizing. However, you can also skew and rotate them. Skewing distorts objects horizontally or vertically, while rotation moves them around their centre point.

Skewing an object

Click twice on the outline of the object you want to skew. CorelDRAW surrounds it with two sorts of handles:

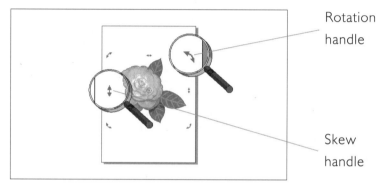

Rotation handle

Skew handle

Re step 2 – to constrain skew to 15° increments, hold down one Ctrl key as you drag.

1 Move the mouse pointer over one of the side handles

2 Hold down the left mouse button, then drag to skew the object

3 Release the mouse button

Re step 3 – if you right-click before you release the left mouse button, CorelDRAW creates a skewed copy of the object, and leaves the original intact.

The same image, skewed

...cont'd

Re step 3 – if you right-click before you release the left mouse button, CorelDRAW creates a rotated copy of the object, and leaves the original intact.

Re step 3 – to constrain rotation to 15° increments, hold down one Ctrl key as you drag.

Rotating an object

1 Click twice on the outline of the object you want to rotate

2 Move the mouse pointer over one of the corner handles, then hold down the left mouse button

3 Drag with a circular motion to rotate the object, then release the mouse button

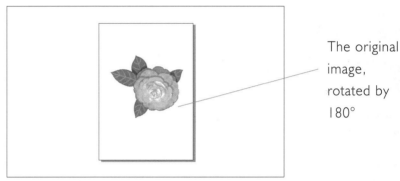

The original image, rotated by 180°

Varying the rotation point

Rotation moves objects around a specific point, normally in the centre of the object. However, if you want you can move this point prior to rotation. Do the following:

Moving the rotation point has a dramatic effect.

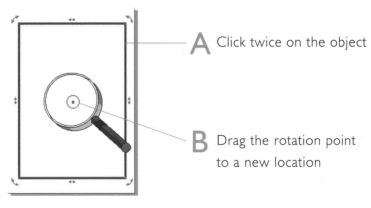

A Click twice on the object

B Drag the rotation point to a new location

C Follow steps 1–3 above

Working with nodes

For ease of use, you can also edit nodes without using the Shape tool.

In any creation tool (e.g. Rectangle, Ellipse or Polygon), move the mouse pointer over the relevant node – it changes to:

Now perform the relevant operation on the node.

To select all nodes within a selected object, ensure the Shape tool is activated. Hold down Ctrl+Shift as you click one node.

There are 3 types of node (Cusp, Smooth and Symmetrical). Control points in each behave slightly differently.

So far, we've looked at techniques which you can use to define or edit *whole* lines or curves. However, CorelDRAW also lets you amend line and curve sections. You can do this because, when you create objects, CorelDRAW inserts 'nodes' automatically. Look at the following Bezier curve:

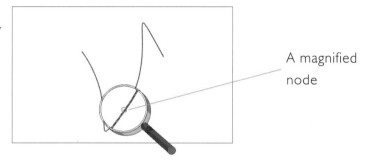

A magnified node

CorelDRAW inserts nodes whenever a curve changes direction (however imperceptibly). Although some nodes are visible when an object is selected with the Pick tool, working with nodes normally involves using the Shape tool. You can drag nodes to reshape curves. You can also add your own nodes or delete existing ones.

Reshaping lines or curves

First, do the following in the Toolbox:

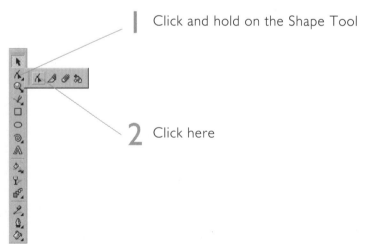

1 Click and hold on the Shape Tool

2 Click here

CorelDRAW 9 in easy steps

...cont'd

 If the existing nodes aren't in the right place, or if there aren't enough, you can create your own – see page 48.

 Nodes have 'control points'. These are points (at the end of dashed lines) which specify how 'segments' (that part of a curve lying between two nodes) are curved. (For an illustration of control points, see page 40.)

 You can also reshape curves by dragging control points. When you do this, vary:

- **the control point's angle**
- **the control point's distance from the node**

to determine the segment's curve.

3 The cursor changes to a black triangle. Place it over the node which you want to move. Left-click and drag the node. When you release the mouse button, the curve is redefined.

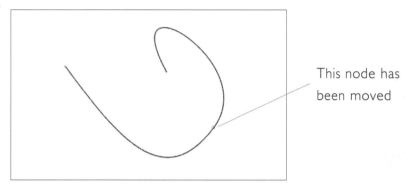

This node has been moved

Another method

Another way to reshape curves is to use the Shape tool to drag the curve itself. This is useful, though less so than working with nodes.

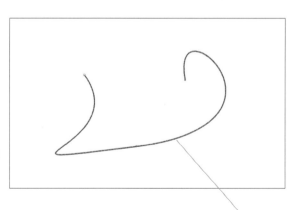

Here, the curve itself has been dragged to a new location

Adding and deleting nodes

If you can't reshape a curve in the way you want by using the existing nodes/control points, or by simply dragging directly on the curve itself, you need to add one or more nodes. Fortunately, this is easy to do. You can also delete nodes.

Adding a node

Re step 2 in 'Adding a node', sometimes CorelDRAW inserts multiple nodes, the better to redefine the line/curve.

1. Ensure the Shape Tool is activated (if it isn't, carry out steps 1–2 on page 46)

2. Double-click the location in the curve where you want the new node inserted

Deleting single node

Deleting nodes is a useful procedure for the following reasons:

- it diminishes the time it takes CorelDRAW to redraw the screen

- it reduces printing time

- the object which contains the nodes often appears smoother

Carry out the following steps:

You can use the Shape tool to marquee-select multiple nodes. To do this, see page 26 (in the instructions under 'Using marquees', substitute Shape Tool for Pick Tool).

1. Ensure the Shape Tool is activated (if it isn't, carry out steps 1–2 on page 46)

2. Double-click the node(s) you want to remove

Deleting multiple nodes

1. Ensure the Shape Tool is activated (if it isn't, carry out steps 1–2 on page 46)

You can also select multiple nodes by holding down Shift as you click them.

2. Select the relevant nodes

3. Click this icon – ▬ – in the Property Bar

Rotating/skewing nodes

A useful feature is the ability to rotate or skew curve nodes. This can produce unique effects.

Rotating/skewing a node

1 Ensure the Shape Tool is activated (if it isn't, carry out steps 1–2 on page 46)

2 Select the relevant node(s) along the curve you want to skew

3 Click this icon – – in the Property Bar

CorelDRAW now surrounds the curve with rotation/skew handles:

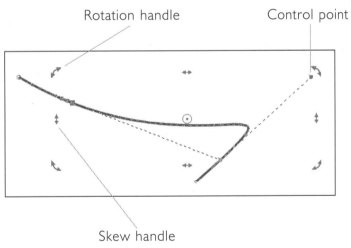

Rotation handle   Control point

Skew handle

4 Follow the relevant procedures on pages 44–45 to rotate or skew the curve

---

 If you're resizing curve segments (see 'Other actions' on page 50), the selected nodes are surrounded with 8 stretch handles. Drag any of these to resize specific curve parts.

 To control how smooth the curve is (see 'Other Actions' on page 50), click the arrow to the right of the box. Do the following:

Drag the slider to the right to increase smoothness, to the left to decrease it

Other node tips

You can carry out the actions listed under 'Reshaping rectangles/circles' simply by moving the Shape tool cursor over a node, double-clicking and dragging.

However, if you want to reshape squares/rectangles and circles/ellipses in more depth, you have to convert them to curves first. To do this, select the object(s), then press Ctrl+Q. Finally, use any of the techniques discussed on pages 46–49 to amend the objects' nodes.

If you're aligning nodes, a dialog launches. Choose any combination of Align Horizontal, Align Vertical or Align Control Points (if available). Click OK.

The following tips should help you get the most out of using nodes.

Reshaping rectangles/circles

Objects created with the use of the Freehand and Bezier tools can be reshaped using the techniques discussed on pages 46–49. However, the extent to which you can amend the following objects with the Shape tool is restricted:

Squares/rectangles   the corners can be rounded

Circles/ellipses   they can be turned into arcs and wedges

Other actions

The Property Bar (when the Shape tool is active) can be used to carry out some fairly intricate node operations on pre-selected nodes. The next illustration shows some of these:

Joins start and   Splits   Aligns
end nodes   curves   nodes

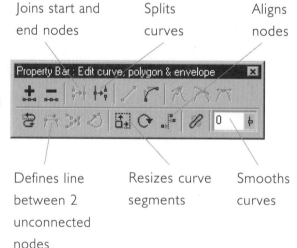

Defines line   Resizes curve   Smooths
between 2   segments   curves
unconnected
nodes

These are largely self-explanatory (but see the DON'T FORGET tips on this and the previous page for more information).

Basic text work

In this chapter, you'll learn how to create Artistic and Paragraph text. You'll also learn how to change basic text formatting (typefaces, type sizes, alignment, spacing and shift/rotation) with and without the use of CorelDRAW's Text editor. Finally, you'll discover how to use various text shortcuts to make working with text even easier.

Covers

Chapter Four

The Text tool

CorelDRAW lets you work with text – a vital component of design work – with the Text tool. You can use the Text tool to enter two kinds of text:

Artistic text

Artistic text is designed to handle relatively short amounts of text. It's the most artistically versatile, and the quickest to use because it's more intuitive: if you want, you can simply click where you need the text to be inserted and start typing straight away.

Use artistic text for single lines of text (e.g. titles or headings), or if you want to apply any of CorelDRAW's special effects (e.g. drop shadow) to text.

Paragraph text

Paragraph text, on the other hand, adopts a more structured approach: text is created in frames. These allow features such as columns, drop caps and tabs/indents which are missing in artistic text.

Use paragraph text for large, formalised blocks of text.

Features in common...

Whichever text type you use, certain features are held in common. For instance, you can:

- amend the typeface and type size

- amend the style (bold, italic etc.) and alignment

- adjust the spacing (between lines, words and characters)

- carry out kerning (reposition characters within words)

- carry out a spell and grammar check

- apply formatting to individual characters within words

Creating artistic text

Creating artistic text is easy from the Toolbox. Carry out the following actions:

Click here

Re step 2 – when you need a new line, press Enter.

2 Left-click in your document where you want the text to appear, then start typing

3 When you've finished typing in text, click the Pick tool in the Toolbox

When you create text in this way, CorelDRAW applies default formatting characteristics (for instance, a standard typeface).
You can easily change these later.

A zoomed view of Artistic text

Creating paragraph text

Creating paragraph text is almost as easy as artistic text. First turn to the Toolbox and do the following:

 **By default, Paragraph text frames are fixed: if you type in more text than the frame can hold, the surplus text does not display. If, however, you want the frame to resize itself to fit the text you type, do the following.**

Press Ctrl+J. In the box on the left of the Options dialog, double-click Text. Select Paragraph. On the right of the dialog, select Expand and shrink paragraph text frames to fit text. Click OK.

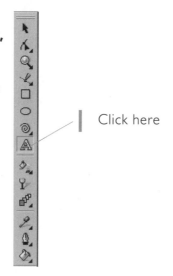

Click here

 Re step 4 – don't press Enter to start a new line. Only press Enter if you want to start a new paragraph.

2 Left-click in your document where you want the text to appear

3 Hold down the left mouse button and drag out a frame. Release the button

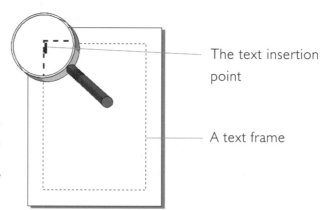

The text insertion point

A text frame

4 Start typing straight away. When you've finished typing, click the Pick tool in the Toolbox.

Changing the typeface

Re step 2 – with both Artistic and Paragraph text, you can select:

- **individual characters**
- **words**
- **whole paragraphs**

CorelDRAW makes applying a new typeface (font) to text easy and convenient. Carry out the following steps:

1 Follow step 1 on page 54

2 Use standard Windows techniques to select the text whose formatting you want to amend

3 Pull down the Text menu and click Format Text

This is the Artistic text version of the Format Text dialog.
(The Paragraph text version has more tabs.)

4 Make sure this tab is active

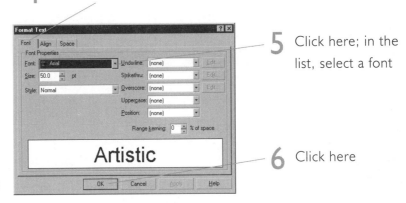

5 Click here; in the list, select a font

6 Click here

If the Text toolbar isn't on-screen, right-click any other toolbar and click Text in the menu.

Using the Text toolbar
Many of the text operations described in this chapter can be undertaken with the use of the Text toolbar.

If you're unsure about the function of a button, move the mouse pointer over it; a HELP bubble launches – e.g:

Underline

1 Click here

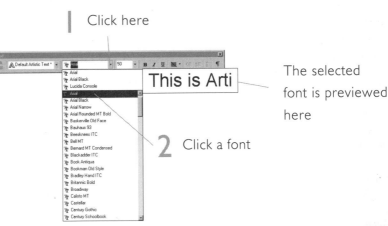

This is Arti

2 Click a font

The selected font is previewed here

Changing the type size

Printed text is usually measured in points. When you want to make text bigger or smaller, you change the point size. You can do this in increments of 0.001 pt. Do the following:

Re step 2 – with both Artistic and Paragraph text, you can select:
- **individual characters**
- **words**
- **whole paragraphs**

1 Follow step 1 on page 54

2 Use standard Windows techniques to select the text whose formatting you want to amend

3 Pull down the Text menu and click Format Text

4 Make sure this tab is active

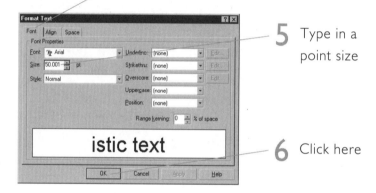

5 Type in a point size

6 Click here

You can also increase paragraph text size with the mouse.

Activate the Pick tool in the Toolbox. Click the paragraph text frame. Move the mouse pointer over a corner handle. Hold down Alt and drag in or out; the frame *and* the text are resized.

(If you omit Alt, only the frame is resized.)

Using the Text toolbar

You can also alter point sizes with the use of the Text toolbar. Do the following:

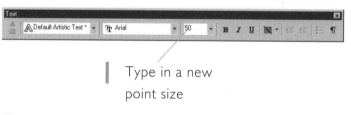

1 Type in a new point size

2 Press Enter

Applying text effects

You can apply a variety of additional effects. You can:

- embolden, *italicise*, <u>underline</u> or ~~strikethru~~ text

- make text subscript or superscript

- change text to ALL CAPS or SMALL CAPS

Do the following:

Re step 2 – with both Artistic and Paragraph text, you can select:
- **individual characters**
- **words**
- **whole paragraphs**

This is the Paragraph text version of the Format Text dialog.
   (The Artistic text version has fewer tabs.)

Re step 5 – some fonts don't support italicisation and/or emboldening.

1 Follow step 1 on page 54

2 Use standard Windows techniques to select the text whose formatting you want to amend

3 Pull down the Text menu and click Format Text

4 Make sure this tab is active

5 Click here; in the list, choose a style option

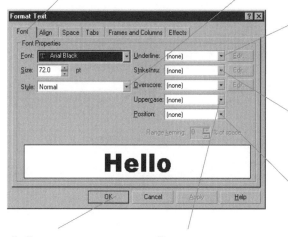

6 Click here; choose an underline option

7 Click here; choose a strikethru option

8 Click here; choose Subscript or Superscript

10 Click here

9 Click here; choose All Caps or Small Caps

Aligning text

You can also set vertical alignment for paragraph text. Select the text. Type Ctrl+T. Click the Frames and Columns tab. Click an option in the Vertical justification field. Click OK.

You can apply the following horizontal alignments to text:

Left
Artistic text aligns to the right of the insertion point; paragraph text is flush with the left frame margin.

Center
Artistic text centres itself around the insertion point; paragraph text aligns between the left/right frame edge.

Right
Artistic text aligns to the left of the insertion point; paragraph text is flush with the right frame margin.

Full Justify
Text is right and left justified.

Force Justify (or Force Full)
Text is stretched to achieve right *and* left justification.

Re step 2 – with both Artistic and Paragraph text, selecting individual characters or words is (in terms of alignment) the same as selecting the whole paragraph.

1 Follow step 1 on page 54

2 Use standard Windows techniques to select the text whose formatting you want to amend

3 Pull down the Text menu and click Format Text

4 Ensure this tab is active

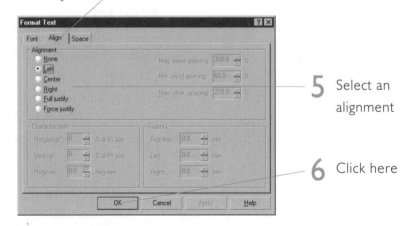

5 Select an alignment

6 Click here

...cont'd

You can also use the Property Bar to carry out the following changes:
- **adjusting the typeface/type size**
- **specifying text alignment**
- **adding/removing Bold, Italic and Underline**

For the first two, see the relevant 'Using the Text Toolbar' sections. For the third, click these icons:

 Bold

I **Italic**

U **Underline**

The paragraph text frames display as boxes here because they have been selected with the Pick Tool.

Using the Text Toolbar

You can also align text with the help of the Text Toolbar.

Follow steps 1–2 on page 58, then carry out the following steps:

Click here

2 In the drop-down list, select an alignment

Alignment in action

The next illustration provides examples of the several types of alignment as applied to paragraph text.

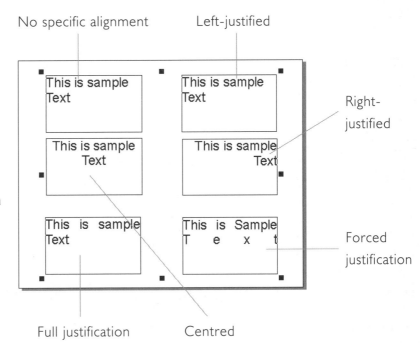

No specific alignment

Left-justified

Right-justified

Forced justification

Full justification

Centred

Adjusting spacing

In typography, line spacing is known as leading (pronounced 'ledding').

Re step 2 – with both Artistic and Paragraph text, selecting individual characters or words is (in terms of spacing) the same as selecting the whole paragraph.

With Paragraph text, you can also specify the spacing before and/or after paragraphs (as a % of character height). Follow steps 1–4, then type in the relevant % in the Before paragraph: or After paragraph: fields, as appropriate. Finally, carry out step 9.

In CorelDRAW, you can amend the spacing between:

- characters
- words
- lines

Character and word-spacing adjustments are measured as percentages of the size of one space character in the relevant font. By default, however, CorelDRAW sets the spacing between lines as a percentage of the character height. You can, though, choose to use different units: you can define line spacing in points, or as a percentage of the point size.

Amending character, word or line spacing

1 Follow step 1 on page 54

2 Use standard Windows techniques to select the text whose formatting you want to amend

3 Pull down the Text menu and click Format Text

4 Make sure this tab is active

5 Type in a new % character adjustment

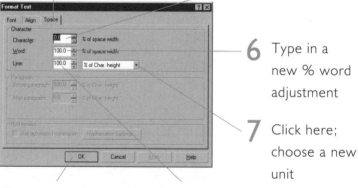

6 Type in a new % word adjustment

7 Click here; choose a new unit

9 Click here

8 Type in a new % line adjustment

Shifting and rotating text

The baseline is the lowest point reached by characters (excluding lower strokes) such as 'a'.

CorelDRAW lets you adjust the position of text relative to the baseline. You can:

- amend text vertically/ horizontally relative to the baseline

- rotate text in relation to the baseline

Do the following:

1 Follow step 1 on page 54

Horizontal and vertical shift are measured as a percentage of the relevant point size, text rotation in degrees.

2 Use standard Windows techniques to select the text whose formatting you want to amend

3 Pull down the Text menu and click Format Text

4 Ensure this tab is active

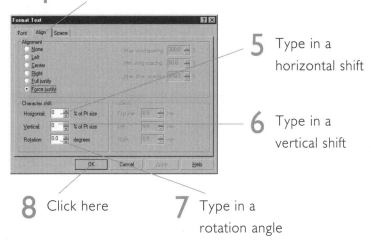

5 Type in a horizontal shift

6 Type in a vertical shift

Re step 7 – you can enter minus rotations e.g. -45°. Doing so produces clockwise, as opposed to anticlockwise, rotation.

8 Click here

7 Type in a rotation angle

Examples:

T   he first character has been shifted horizontally

T
   he first character has been shifted vertically

↖   he first character has been rotated

Shift and rotation in action

The dedicated text editor

With CorelDRAW, as we've seen, you can edit text in situ. Often, this is desirable. By selecting the Text tool and clicking the relevant text, you can begin adding to it or changing it immediately. However, there are times when it's convenient to use a separate text editor.

One reason for this is that using the editor is quicker: you don't have to wait for the screen to redraw each time you make a correction or addition. Another is that the editor provides access to the Format Text dialog we've been using in this chapter. And it also has its own mini Text toolbar which you can use to set a new typeface/type size or change the text style or alignment.

 Text in the editor isn't WYSIWYG ('What You See Is What You Get'). For example, point size increases don't display accurately.

Launching the editor

1 Select the relevant text (either with the Pick tool or the Text tool)

2 Press Ctrl+Shift+T

 If you want to format your text, click:

 Format Text...

then complete the Format Text dialog in line with earlier topics.
  Finally, carry out step 4.

The editor's toolbar

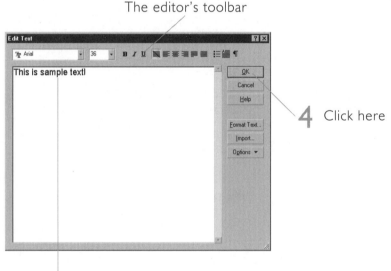

4 Click here

3 Amend the text as necessary

Text shortcuts

CorelDRAW allows you to:

- increase/decrease type sizes incrementally

- set the level of the increment for both increases and decreases

- increase/decrease type sizes relative to the next highest or lowest point size listed in the Font List

 **Using these shortcuts can save you a lot of time and effort.**

Incrementing type sizes

Select the text you want to change. Ensure Number Lock is enabled (by clicking the Num Lock key). Now do the following:

> Hold down one Ctrl key and press 8 on the numerical keypad to the right of your keyboard. Repeat as often as necessary

CorelDRAW adds one point to the existing text size.

Decrementing type sizes

Select the text you want to change. Ensure Number Lock is enabled (by clicking the Num Lock key). Now do the following:

> Hold down one Ctrl key and press 2 on the numerical keypad to the right of your keyboard. Repeat as often as necessary

CorelDRAW subtracts one point from the existing text size.

Specifying the increment/decrement

You can also specify the amount of the increment/ decrement.

Press Ctrl+J; the Options dialog launches. Do the following:

> In the list of categories on the left, click Text. In the Keyboard Text Increment box, enter a new increment (in whole points). Click OK

Increasing type sizes relative to the Font List

Select the text you want to change. Ensure Number Lock is enabled (by clicking the Num Lock key). Now do the following:

Repeat step 1 as often as necessary.

| Hold down one Ctrl key and press 6 on the numerical keypad to the right of your keyboard

CorelDRAW applies the next highest size in the Font List:

The current type size is 72 points

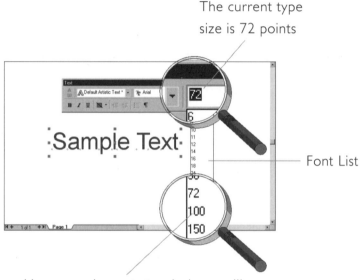

Font List

Here, carrying out step 1 above will increase the type size to 100 points

Decreasing type sizes relative to the Font List

Select the text you want to change. Ensure Number Lock is enabled (by clicking the Num Lock key). Now do the following:

Repeat step 1 as often as necessary.

| Hold down one Ctrl key and press 4 on the numerical keypad to the right of your keyboard

CorelDRAW applies the next lowest point size in the Font List (in the above example, 50).

Advanced text work

CorelDRAW has a variety of advanced text features. In this chapter, you'll learn how to set tabs and indents; work with text columns; flow text between paragraph frames; and carry out kerning. Finally, you'll format single characters; flow text around shapes; create and apply text styles; proofread text; and make text three-dimensional.

Covers

Chapter Five

Using tabs

You can only apply tabs to paragraph, not artistic text.

One feature of paragraph, as opposed to artistic text is the ability to impose tabs and indents. Tabs and indents are related features in that they both control the extent to which the first lines of paragraphs align with the left margin. Indents, however, go much further than this. You can also use them to control the alignment of subsequent lines with the left margin, and the overall alignment with the right margin.

Imposing tabs – the dialog route

1 Follow step 1 on page 53

2 Click anywhere in the paragraph for which you want to define tabs (or select more than one paragraph)

Re steps 5 and 6 – these are alternatives.

To impose tabs at regular intervals, follow step 5. To add a single tab, perform step 6.

3 Pull down the Format menu and click Format Text

4 Ensure this tab is active

5 Type in the interval (e.g. 0.35) then click Set tabs every

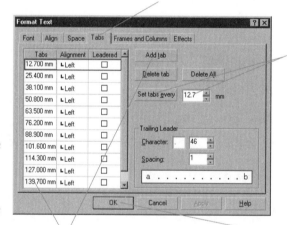

It's a good idea to use indents, rather than tabs, to align even the 1st lines of paragraphs. This is because tabs have to be physically inserted for each paragraph, whereas indents can be applied with a single command.

6 Click Add Tab; type in details of the new tab. Press Enter

7 Click here to apply the tab settings

To make text conform to the tabs you've imposed, place the cursor at the start of the relevant paragraph. Press Tab as often as required.

Imposing tabs with the Paragraph Text ruler

A quicker and more convenient way to set tabs is to use a special version of the ruler which appears over paragraph text:

Normally, tab marks don't display, but you can make them visible – and also other features e.g. paragraph marks:

¶

Pull down the Text menu and select Show Non-Printing Characters.

The Paragraph Text ruler is only visible if the relevant text has been selected with the Text Tool.

Tab/indent ruler

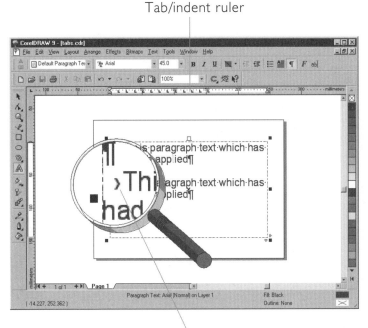

Magnified view of tab mark

You can use the ruler in the following ways:

1. To add a new tab, simply click the ruler where you want the tab to appear.

2. To remove a tab, left-click it. Hold down the mouse button and drag it off the ruler. When you release the button, it disappears.

3. To move an existing tab to a new position, left-click it. Hold down the mouse button and drag it to its new location. Release the button to confirm the move.

Using indents

You can only indent paragraph, not artistic text.

For reasons set out in the HOT TIP on page 66, indents are the preferred solution for aligning paragraph text. They're easier to apply than tabs, and more convenient.

You can indent:

- the first line of one or more paragraphs

- all lines (excluding the first) of one or more paragraphs (CorelDRAW calls this a Left or Rest of Lines indent)

- one or more paragraphs from the right frame margin

You can apply these in any permutations.

Applying indents via a dialog

1 Follow step 1 on page 53

2 Click anywhere in the paragraph for which you want to define indents (or select more than one paragraph)

3 Pull down the Format menu and click Format Text

4 Ensure this tab is active

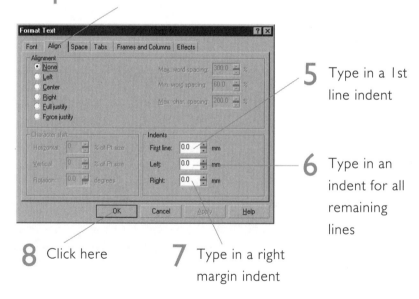

5 Type in a 1st line indent

6 Type in an indent for all remaining lines

8 Click here

7 Type in a right margin indent

Applying indents via the ruler

You can use the special ruler which appears over paragraph text to impose indents, too. The next illustration shows the ruler, together with sample indents:

Tab/indent ruler

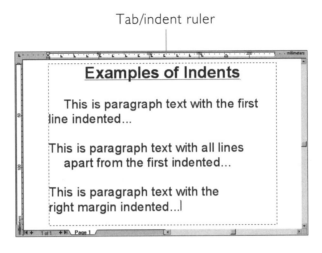

Examples of Indents

This is paragraph text with the first line indented...

This is paragraph text with all lines apart from the first indented...

This is paragraph text with the right margin indented...

1 Follow step 1 on page 53

2 Click anywhere in the paragraph for which you want to define indents (or select more than one paragraph)

3 Drag any of the buttons in the illustration below to implement the required indents:

If you drag on the lower section of the Rest of Lines marker:

—Here

CorelDRAW moves the left indent for all lines in the specified paragraph(s).

First line indent   Right indent

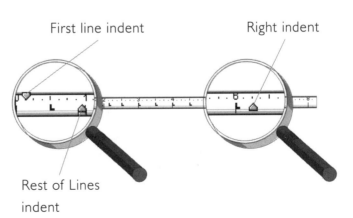

Rest of Lines indent

Applying columns to text

Another feature which is unique to paragraph, as opposed to artistic text is the ability to have CorelDRAW format text in columns.

You can do either of the following:

- impose equal-sized columns (in which case you simply tell CorelDRAW how many you require)

- specify columns of varying width

By default, CorelDRAW assumes you want the former.

Imposing columns

First, select the paragraph text frame, either with the Pick tool or the Text tool. Then pull down the Text menu and click Format Text. Now perform steps 1–2 below. If you want columns of varying width, also perform steps 3–4. Finally, carry out step 5:

| Ensure this tab is active

2 Type in the no. of columns you need

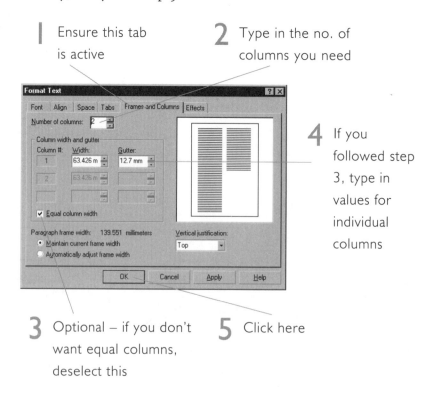

4 If you followed step 3, type in values for individual columns

3 Optional – if you don't want equal columns, deselect this

5 Click here

Linking frames

In earlier chapters, we mentioned that paragraph text is contained within frames. Frames are boxes which add useful structure to the text they contain. However, they also permit one further operation: you can have text flow from one frame to another. CorelDRAW achieves this by 'linking' frames.

The flow is dynamic. In other words, if you change the size of one frame (or resize the text), the contents of the second update automatically.

Linking frames

Activate the Pick tool and click the frame which has surplus text. Then do the following:

You can also use this procedure to link a text frame with another on a different page.
  Simply use the Page Forward or Page Backward controls in the Page Counter (see page 10) to move to the new page before you define or fill the second frame.

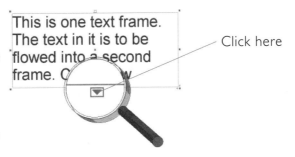

Click here

You can now define a further frame, and repeat the process.

The cursor changes into a representation of a page. Left-click and hold down the mouse button. Drag to define an additional frame which you want to receive some or all of the overflow (or click inside an empty frame you've already created). When you release the button, CorelDRAW flows the text into the second frame:

If the second frame also contains too much text to display, CorelDRAW displays this:

on the lower frame edge.

This indicates that the frame is linked

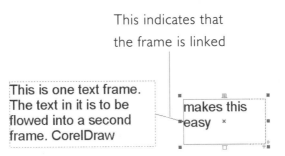

Editing individual characters

In Chapter 3, we looked at how to use the Shape Tool to edit nodes as a way of redrawing curves and lines. However, you can also use the Shape Tool to edit one or more text characters. You can:

- adjust letter spacing (i.e. carry out kerning)

- apply formatting (e.g. change the typeface/type size)

Kerning text

Kerning is the reduction of space between specific pairs of letters to compensate for the inherent awkwardness of their shapes. In the next illustration, the 'A' and 'v' are too far apart to be aesthetically pleasing:

The answer is to move the 'A' nearer to the 'v'.

Refer to the Toolbox and do the following:

You can add drop caps to paragraph text:

Drop cap

Click the Text tool. Select one or more paragraphs. Press Ctrl+T. In the Format Text dialog, click the Effects tab. Select Drop cap in the Effect Type: field.

Now choose a drop cap type. In the Dropped lines: field, type in the number of lines you want the drop cap to descend. In the Distance from text: box, type in a horizontal separation. Finally, click OK.

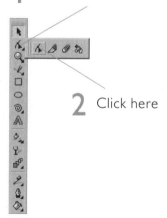

1 Click and hold on the Shape Tool

2 Click here

...cont'd

To select more than one node (and therefore more than one character), hold down one Shift key as you click them.

3 To kern an individual character in artistic text, click the text; to kern an individual character in paragraph text, click anywhere in the frame

4 Click the node to the left of the character you want to edit; CorelDRAW fills it to show it's selected e.g:

5 Drag the node to the left or right to kern the character

The end result:

Kerning has taken place

Formatting individual characters

To change the formatting of an individual character in artistic text, click the text; to change the formatting of an individual character in paragraph text, click anywhere in the frame. Then, in either case, click the node to the left of the character you want to edit; CorelDRAW fills it to show it's selected.

Now follow any of the text formatting procedures discussed in Chapter 4 (bear in mind that some of them – e.g. alignment – affect the *whole* of the word or paragraph in which one or more nodes have been selected).

Here, the 'A' has had a new typeface/type size imposed

Working with text styles

Styles are collections of associated formatting commands which can be applied to text with a single mouse click, thereby saving a lot of time and effort. They also ensure a consistent look and feel within documents.

CorelDRAW comes with one pre-defined artistic text style.

Creating a text style

1 Create an artistic text string or a paragraph text frame, then apply the relevant formatting

2 Right-click over the text

3 Click here

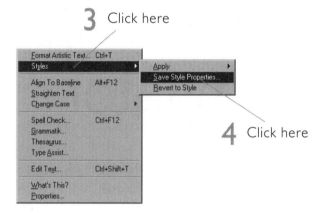

4 Click here

Re step 6 – to deselect an option, click here:

so that the tick disappears.

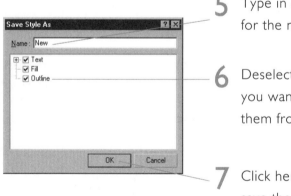

5 Type in a name for the new style

6 Deselect any of these if you want to exclude them from the new style

7 Click here to save the style

Applying styles

Once you've created a style, applying it to text is very easy. The procedure for both artistic and paragraph text is the same.

1 With either the Pick tool or the Text tool, select the text you want to apply the style to

2 Right-click over the text

This menu changes according to whether the relevant text was selected with the Text or Pick Tool.

3 Click here

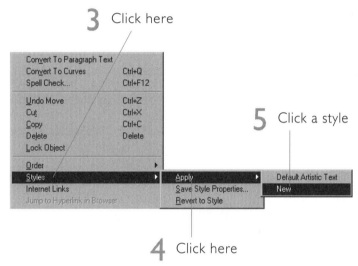

5 Click a style

4 Click here

More styles

If, in step 5, the needed style isn't listed, click More Styles instead, then carry out the following additional steps:

Steps 6–7 are required if you've created more styles than can display in the sub-menu associated with step 5.

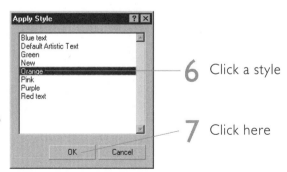

6 Click a style

7 Click here

Fitting text to a path

You can have artistic text conform to a path. In this sense, a path is any drawing object which has the requisite shape. For example, you can have CorelDRAW align text automatically along the perimeter of a rectangle, ellipse or polygon. When you do this, you can determine:

- the text orientation relative to the path (the extent to which the characters are rotated)

- the vertical position/alignment of the text (relative to the text baseline)

- in the case of closed (filled) objects, the horizontal alignment of the text i.e. you specify which side of the path text aligns with

Carry out the following steps, as appropriate:

1 With the Pick Tool, select the object you want to align the text on

2 Hold down Shift and select the text

3 Pull down the Text menu and do the following:

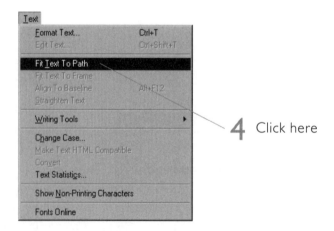

4 Click here

...cont'd

You can also type directly onto open or closed paths.

Activate the Text Tool. Place the cursor near to the object along which you want the text aligned. The cursor becomes:

Left-click once and start typing.

To customise directly aligned text, carry out steps 1–8, as appropriate.

To have the text transposed to the opposite side of the current path, click this button in the Property Bar:

Here, the end result is:

~~Sample~~

CorelDRAW aligns the object and text:

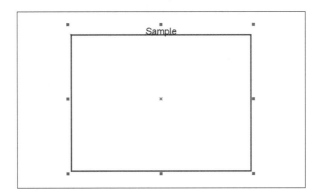

Customising the operation

It now remains to customise the object/text interaction.

Refer to the Property Bar and carry out the following additional steps, as appropriate:

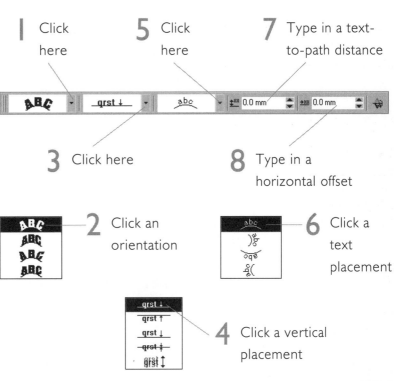

1 Click here

5 Click here

7 Type in a text-to-path distance

3 Click here

8 Type in a horizontal offset

2 Click an orientation

6 Click a text placement

4 Click a vertical placement

Spell-checking text

CorelDRAW lets you proofread text in a variety of ways. You can:

- carry out a spell-check

- run a grammar check (see page 80)

- run the Thesaurus to find synonyms (see page 81)

Launching a spell-check

Repeat steps 4–7 for as many incorrect words as are flagged.

| Select the relevant text with the Pick or Text Tool

2 Press Ctrl+F12, then carry out the following steps, as appropriate

Re step 4 – if the flagged word isn't wrong and you want the Spell Checker to recognise it in future, omit steps 4–5. Instead, click the Add button – the word is inserted into a special 'user' dictionary, WT9UK.UWL.

(Alternatively, if you only want the correct word recognised in this checking session, follow step 7.)

4 The 1st unrecognised word is flagged; if it's wrong, correct it here then click Replace

6 Click here to leave the flagged word as it is

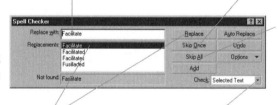

7 Or here to ignore *all* instances (in *this* session)

5 Or click any valid correction, then Replace

3 Click here; choose the extent of the spell-check from the list

When the spell-check is complete, CorelDRAW launches this message. Do the following:

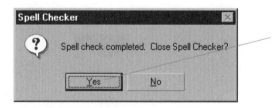

8 Click here

Automatic spell-checking

You can also spell-check text on-the-fly, as you enter or amend text. CorelDRAW is automatically set up to do this. When automatic correction is in force, CorelDRAW flags any unrecognised words with a red underline.

The spell-checker also flags incorrect capitals, duplicated words, hyphenation errors, 'a/an' errors and other typographical mistakes.

Do the following:

1 Select the text with the Text Tool

2 Right-click any flagged word, then do ONE of the following:

3 CorelDRAW provides alternatives; if one is correct, click it to have it replace the original word

To add the flagged word to your user dictionary, click Spelling. In the Spell Checker dialog, click the Add button. Then click Yes to terminate the spell check.

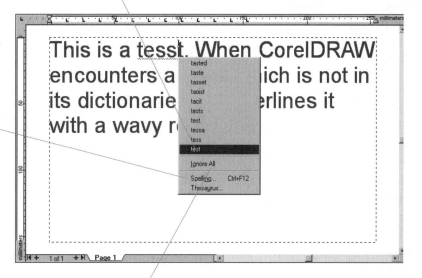

This is a tesst. When CorelDRAW encounters a [word] which is not in its dictionaries [und]erlines it with a wavy r[ed]

tasted
taste
tasset
taoist
tacit
tests
test.
tessa
tess
tèst
Ignore All
Spelling...   Ctrl+F12
Thesaurus...

1 of 1   Page 1

4 If you want the flagged word to stand, click here

Disabling on-the-fly checking
Sometimes, automatic spell-checking is intrusive. To turn it off, pull down the Tools menu and click Options. On the left of the dialog, double-click Text, then click Spelling. Deselect Perform automatic spell checking. Click OK.

Grammar-checking text

The Grammar Checker also detects spelling errors.

CorelDRAW has an inbuilt Grammar Checker. When you use it to check text, CorelDRAW subjects the text to collections of style rules known as checking styles. There are 11 of these, organised into writing categories. Examples are:

Spelling Plus	finds spelling errors and flags *simple* grammatical infringements
Quick Check	the default. Suitable for most documents
Fiction	accepts informal language, with plenty of artistic license
Formal Memo or Letter	for formal/legal documents; rules are strictly adhered to

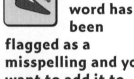

Repeat steps 4, 5 and 6 for as many incorrect expressions as are flagged.

Running a grammar-check

1 Select the text with the Text Tool

2 Pull down the Text menu and click Writing Tools, Grammatik

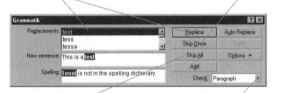

4 The 1st unrecognised expression is flagged; click a valid correction, then Replace

5 Click here to accept the flagged expression

6 Or here to ignore *all* occurrences (in this session only)

3 Click here; choose the extent of the grammar-check from the list

Re step 4 – if a correct word has been flagged as a misspelling and you want to add it to WT9UK.UWL so that it's recognised in future, omit step 4. Instead, click Add.

(Alternatively, if you only want the correct word recognised in this checking session, follow step 6.)

When the check is complete, CorelDRAW launches a special message. Click Yes to return to your document.

Searching for synonyms

You can have CorelDRAW search for synonyms for a specified word. Once you've found the synonym you want to use, you can have it inserted into your document so that it automatically replaces the original word.

1 In artistic or paragraph text, select the relevant word with the Text Tool

2 Pull down the Text menu and do the following:

Re step 6 – when you select a synonym, a separate section appears on the right of the dialog:

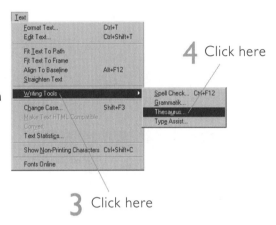

4 Click here

3 Click here

This lists further definitions; if none of the synonyms so far found are suitable, don't carry out step 7. Instead, double-click one of the extra definitions.

(If you select another synonym, CorelDRAW opens yet another section in the dialog.)

Now carry out the following steps, as appropriate:

5 Double-click the appropriate definition

7 Click here to have it replace the original word

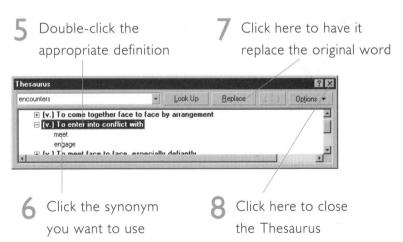

6 Click the synonym you want to use

8 Click here to close the Thesaurus

Carrying out text searches

You can have CorelDRAW search for specific text within the active document. If you want, you can make the search case-specific i.e. searching for 'MATCH' will not find:

- Match

- match

You can also have CorelDRAW replace the words it flags with the replacements of your choice.

Select Match Case to make search or search-and-replace operations case-specific.

Finding text

1 Pull down the Edit menu and click Find and Replace, Find Text

2 Type in the search text

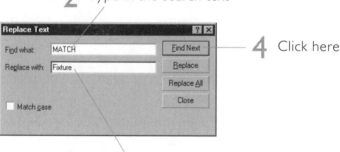

3 Click here – repeat as often as necessary

After step 4, click Replace to have the replacement text substituted for the original. Repeat as often as necessary. Press Esc to close the dialog when you've finished.

Finding and replacing text

1 Pull down the Edit menu and click Find and Replace, Replace Text

2 Type in the search text

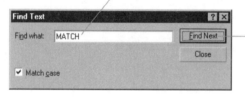

4 Click here

You can also opt to have all instances of the search text replaced automatically. Ignore step 4. Instead, click Replace All.

3 Type in replacement text

The Outline Tool

This chapter shows you how to apply and customise object outlines. You'll learn how to apply pre-defined outlines, specify various outline settings (width, colour and style) and add arrows to line ends. You'll also create your own arrow and line designs, customise line endings and use CorelDRAW's calligraphic pen. Finally, you'll specify blanket outline defaults for objects (graphic and/or text) you create in all future CorelDRAW sessions.

Covers

Chapter Six

An overview

Every object you create in CorelDRAW automatically has a default outline. You can change this, if you want. Outline features you can change include:

- line colour

- line thickness (hairline to thick)

- line shape (slanted or symmetrical)

- line endings (of open, unfilled objects)

- corner endings (of closed, filled objects)

Technically, when you change an object's outline you amend the visible line which follows the object's perimeter. You don't need to concern yourself overly with what is generally, in practice, a fine distinction. However, you should bear in mind one result: if you apply a blank outline to an object (sometimes a worthwhile option), because it isn't visible CorelDRAW regards the object as not having an outline.

You can implement the various outline changes in the following ways:

You can also use the Outline Color dialog to colour outlines.

- by using the Outline Tool and its fly-out

- by using the Outline Pen dialog

- by using the Property Bar

General guidelines
The Outline fly-out provides access to several pre-defined outline settings, and is therefore a convenient shortcut. The Property Bar, like any toolbar, can sit on screen more or less permanently, and is thus preferable if you're carrying out a lot of outline adjustments. However, the Outline Pen dialog is the main channel for working with outlines, if only because it provides the most features and precision.

Working with preset outlines

For how to create default outline properties (so that new objects automatically inherit them), see page 108.

The Outline Tool produces a useful fly-out. If you need to apply outlines to one or more objects quickly and conveniently, and the *precise* thickness of the outline isn't of primary importance, use the Outline fly-out. (You can also use the Outline fly-out to remove outlines from selected objects.)

First, select the object(s) you want to outline. Turn to the Toolbox and carry out step 1 below. Then click one of the additional options detailed in the illustration below:

Points are a unit in typogra-phy.
(72 points are roughly equal to one inch.)

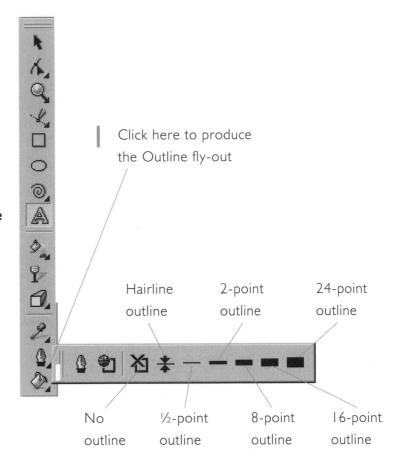

Click here to produce the Outline fly-out

Hairline outline

2-point outline

24-point outline

No outline

½-point outline

8-point outline

16-point outline

Setting outline widths

There are two principal routes to the establishment of *precise* outline widths: the Outline Pen dialog and the Property Bar.

Using the Outline Pen dialog

You can specify a specific outline width from within the Outline Pen dialog. You can also specify which unit you want the width measured in.

First, select the object(s) you want to outline. Launch the Outline Pen dialog. To do this, launch the Outline fly-out (see page 85 for how to do this). Then do the following:

Click here

Now carry out the following steps:

2 Optional – click here and choose a new unit from the list

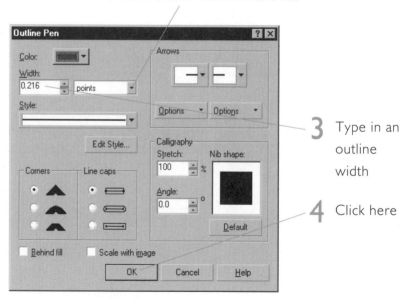

3 Type in an outline width

4 Click here

...cont'd

Using the Property Bar
The Property Bar has convenience on its side: you can keep it on-screen for as long as necessary without it getting in your way, which makes its use perfect if you want to work with a number of outlines.

 If the Property Bar isn't currently on-screen, you can also use a keyboard shortcut to launch it. Simply press Ctrl+Return.

1 If the Property Bar isn't currently on-screen, right-click any toolbar and select Property Bar in the menu

2 Activate the Pick Tool in the on-screen Toolbox

3 Select the object(s) you want to outline

4 Perform step 5, OR steps 6–7

5 Type in a new outline width here

```
x 84.974 m  ↔ 72.447 mm  100.0 %   ⟳ 0.0        °   ⊞    ▭▾ ━▾ ▭▾ ⬡ ⌀ Hairline ▾ 🖳 0
y 132.008   ↕ 50.654 mm  100.0 %
```

6 Click here

| None |
| Hairline |
| 0.5 pt |
| **1.0 pt** |
| 2.0 pt |
| 4.0 pt |
| 8.0 pt |
| 16.0 pt |
| 24.0 pt |

7 Click a preset outline width

Setting outline colours

You can apply colours to outlines in a variety of ways. We'll be looking at the following methods:

- using the Outline Pen dialog

- using the Outline Color dialog

- using on-screen colour palettes

Using the Outline Pen dialog

First select the object(s) whose outlines you want to colour. Then launch the Outline Pen flyout (see page 85 for how to do this). Now carry out the following steps:

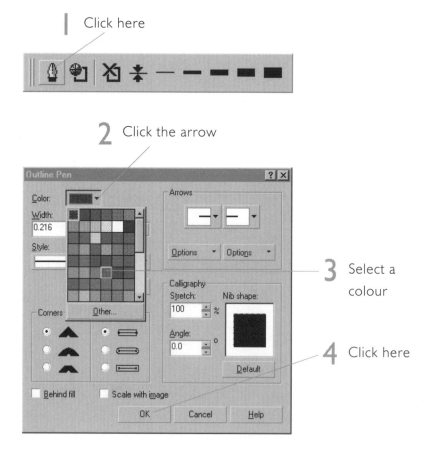

Click here

2 Click the arrow

3 Select a colour

4 Click here

...cont'd

Corel-DRAW supports numerous colour models (ways of describing colours).

To apply a new model, click the Model: field before you carry out step 6 or 7. In the list, select a model.

Colours are defined numerically in various ways – see the tip above.

In the example here, the CMYK model is in use, and colours are therefore defined as permutations of:

- **Cyan (green/blue)**
- **Magenta**
- **Yellow**
- **Black (K)**

Re step 7 – available fields vary with the active colour model.

Using the Outline Color dialog

The Outline Color dialog is a special dialog which allows you to apply outline colours in the following ways:

- by selecting a colour visually

- by selecting a colour numerically

1 Activate the Pick Tool in the on-screen Toolbox

2 Select the object(s) you want to outline

3 Follow step 1 on page 85

4 Click here

Now perform step 5, then 6 OR 7. Finally, carry out step 8:

5 Ensure this tab is active

6 Select a colour

7 Type in numerical components

8 Click here

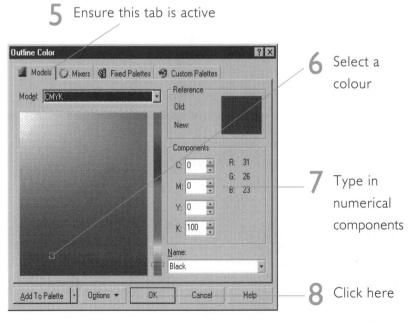

By default, colour palettes display on the right of the screen.

To reposition a palette, click it outside the colour swatches, then drag it to another screen edge.

 If no colour palette is currently visible, pull down the Window menu and click Color Palettes. In the submenu, choose the palette you want to use.

(You can have more than one open at a time.)

 Click here: to expand the active colour palette so more colours are visible.

(To shrink it, click anywhere outside the palette.)

Using colour palettes

First select one or more objects whose outlines you want to colour. Then refer to the on-screen palette – see page 9 if you're not sure of its location, and see the HOT TIP if it isn't currently on screen.

Carry out the following procedure:

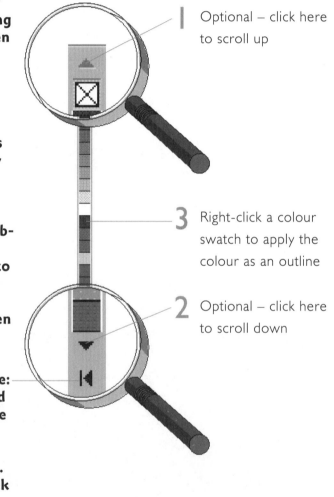

1 Optional – click here to scroll up

3 Right-click a colour swatch to apply the colour as an outline

2 Optional – click here to scroll down

Setting outline styles

CorelDRAW provides a variety of pre-defined line styles (including a solid line) which you can apply as outlines. The numerous options include:

- dotted lines

- dashed lines

- lines with combinations of dots, dashes and spaces, in varying sizes and permutations

You can impose these styles in the following ways:

- by using the Outline Pen dialog

- by using the Property Bar

You can also create your own line styles. You do this by amending existing line styles, specifying which dots in a line are active and inactive. You then:

- save the line style you've created as a new independent style

or

- substitute your new line style for the existing one

Using the Outline Pen dialog

1 Activate the Pick Tool in the on-screen Toolbox

2 Select the object(s) you want to outline

3 Follow step 1 on page 85

4 Click here

5 Click here

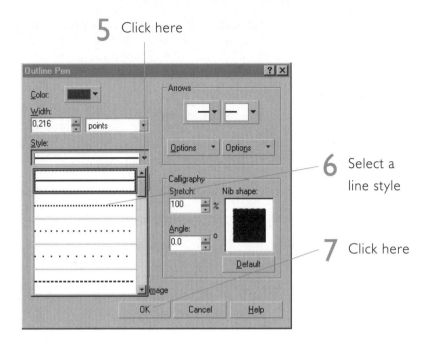

6 Select a
line style

7 Click here

Example:

A spiral, outlined with one out of
approximately 30 line styles

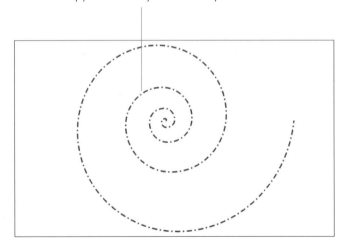

...cont'd

If the Property Bar isn't currently on-screen, you can also use a keyboard shortcut to launch it. Simply press Ctrl+Return.

Using the Property Bar

You can use the Property Bar to apply any of the full range of line styles as outlines (you can also use it to create your own – see page 96):

1 If the Property Bar isn't currently on-screen, right-click any toolbar and select Property Bar in the menu

2 Activate the Pick Tool in the on-screen Toolbox

3 Select the object(s) you want to outline

4 Click here

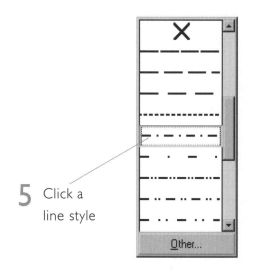

5 Click a line style

Creating line styles

You can customise existing line styles, in order to create your own. You can do this in the following ways:

- using the Outline Pen dialog

- using the Property Bar

Using the Outline Pen dialog

First launch the Outline Pen flyout (see page 85). Now carry out the following steps:

1 Click here

2 Click here; select an existing line style in the list

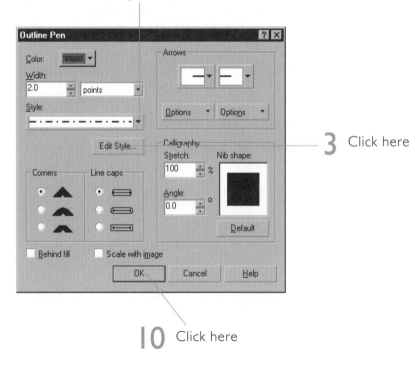

3 Click here

10 Click here

4 Optional – drag the marker
to extend the line

Re step 4 – extending the line ensures that the dots etc. are more widely separated.

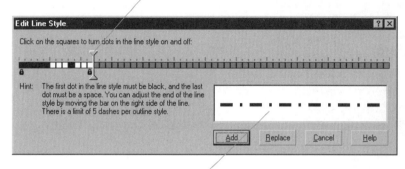

The first square in a line style must be black, and the final one white.

Changes made to your line style
in steps 4-6 are previewed here

5 Click one or more white squares (spaces) to fill them in

6 Click one or more black squares to empty them

Perform step 7 OR 8, as appropriate.

7 Click: Add   to include your completed line style in the list produced in step 2

8 Click: Replace   to substitute your completed line style for the one you selected in step 2

9 Perform step 10 on the facing page

Example:

A customised line style

...cont'd

**If the
Property
Bar isn't
currently
on-screen, you can
also use a keyboard
shortcut to launch
it. Simply press
Ctrl+Return.**

Using the Property Bar

You can use the Property Bar as a useful shortcut to creating your own line style.

1   If the Property Bar isn't currently on-screen, right-click any toolbar and select Property Bar in the menu

2   Activate the Pick Tool in the on-screen Toolbox

3   Select the object(s) you want to outline

4   Click here

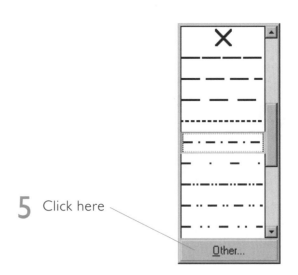

5   Click here

6   Follow steps 4–8 on page 95

Applying outline arrows

You can add arrows to the ends of lines and open curves (CorelDRAW lets you choose from a wide selection of arrow designs) by means of the Outline Pen dialog or the Property Bar.

Using the Outline dialog

First select the line or curve whose ends you want to apply arrows to. Launch the Outline Pen fly-out (see page 85). Now carry out the following, as appropriate:

| Click here

 Re step 2 – the left arrow selector
defines the arrow for the start of your line/curve.

2 Click here to launch the left arrow selector

3 Or click here to launch the right arrow selector

 Re step 3 – the right arrow selector
defines the arrow for the end of your line/curve.

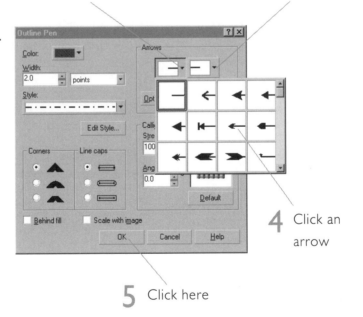

4 Click an arrow

5 Click here

...cont'd

If the Property Bar isn't currently on-screen, you can also use a keyboard shortcut to launch it. Simply press Ctrl+Return.

Using the Property Bar
You can use the Property Bar as a useful shortcut to applying left and right arrows.

1 If the Property Bar isn't currently on-screen, right-click any toolbar and select Property Bar in the menu

2 Activate the Pick Tool in the on-screen Toolbox

3 Select the object(s) you want to outline

4 Click here to launch the left arrow selector

5 Or click here to launch the right arrow selector

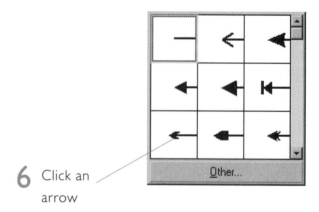

6 Click an arrow

Editing arrows

When you apply arrows to line or curve ends, you're not limited to the arrows CorelDRAW supplies. You can, if you want, edit these to produce your own designs.

When you want to create your own arrow design, it's helpful to base it on the existing design which is nearest to what you want.

Launching the arrow editor

Launch the Outline Pen fly-out (see page 85). Then carry out the following steps, as appropriate:

Click here

2 Perform steps 2–4 on page 97, as appropriate

An arrow has been selected

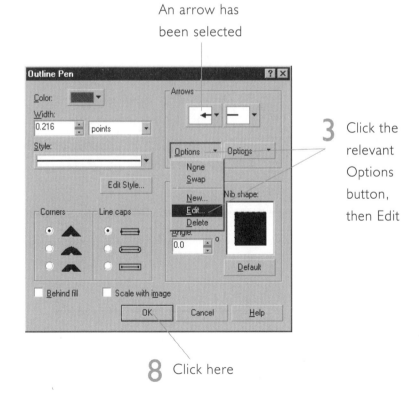

3 Click the relevant Options button, then Edit

8 Click here

4 Drag any of the filled
handles (as appropriate) to
rescale or stretch the arrow

**If you
don't want
a gap
between
the arrow and line,
drag this:
up to the arrow.**

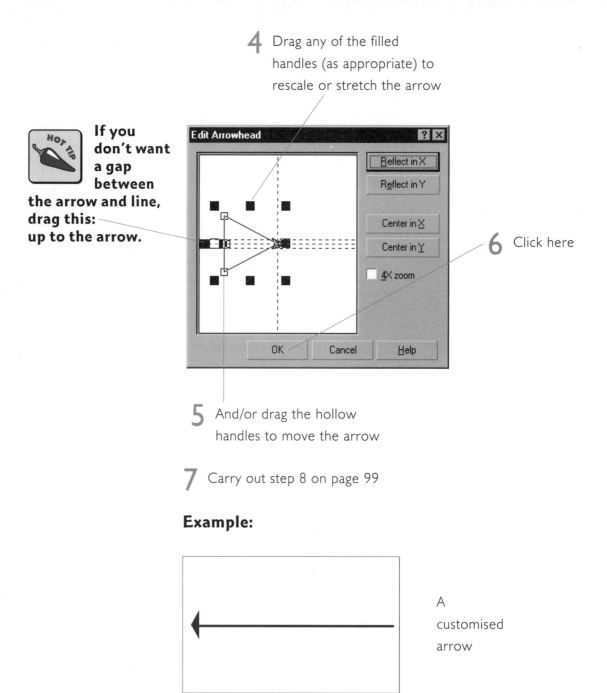

6 Click here

5 And/or drag the hollow
handles to move the arrow

7 Carry out step 8 on page 99

Example:

A
customised
arrow

Configuring polygon corners

CorelDRAW lets you reshape polygon corners. The effects of doing this can be quite subtle, but they are easy to implement.

Corners can be:

Mitered	the default – the corners are pointed
Rounded	self-explanatory
Beveled	the corners are blunt (squared off)

Reshaping polygon corners has more effect in the following circumstances:

- when the object or objects concerned are particularly small

- when the object or objects concerned have a particularly thick line width

Applying a specific corner type

1 Activate the Pick Tool in the on-screen Toolbox

2 Select one or more objects whose corners you want to customise

3 Follow step 1 on page 85

4 Click here

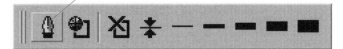

...cont'd

5 Click a corner type

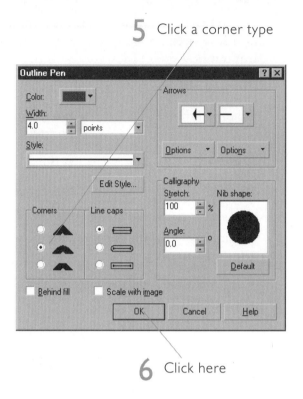

6 Click here

Example:

Magnified view of
pointed corner

Magnified view of
blunt corner

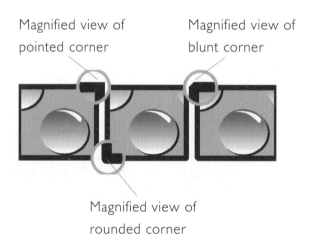

Magnified view of
rounded corner

Configuring line/curve caps

Another way in which you can customise open paths (lines or curves whose start and end points have not been connected) is to specify how their ends are capped.

There are three settings you can choose from:

Square Line	the ends are truncated, and perpendicular to the line or curve
Rounded Line	the cap diameter is equal to the width of the line/curve – as a result, the path is marginally longer
Extended Square Line	the cap is square and extends beyond the line by 50% of the line width – as a result, the line is noticeably longer

Capping lines

1 Activate the Pick Tool in the on-screen Toolbox

2 Select one or more objects whose ends you want to customise

3 Follow step 1 on page 85

4 Click here

5 Click a line cap

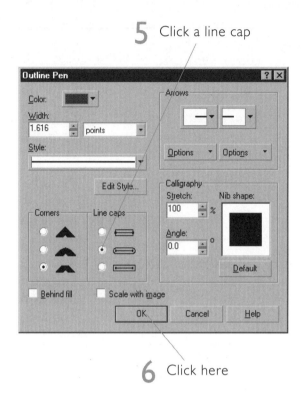

6 Click here

Examples:

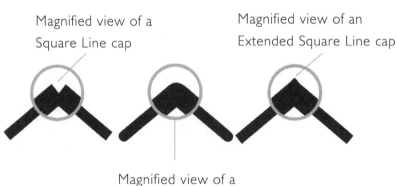

Magnified view of a
Square Line cap

Magnified view of an
Extended Square Line cap

Magnified view of a
Rounded Line cap

Applying calligraphic outlines

You can apply calligraphic effects to outlines. You do this by varying:

The corner shape	see page 101 for details of available shapes
The nib stretch	decreasing the extent of stretch produces the following effects:

- square nibs become rectangles

- round nibs become elliptical

The nib angle	this value determines the angle at which the nib interacts with the drawing surface

You can customise an object's stretch and angle by entering values directly into the Outline Pen dialog. However, you can also do so visually, with the use of the mouse.

Applying a calligraphic outline

1 Activate the Pick Tool in the on-screen Toolbox

2 Select one or more objects to which you want to apply calligraphic effects

3 Follow step 1 on page 85

4 Click here

5 Click a corner style
(to determine the
basic nib shape)

To adjust
the nib
stretch
visually,
ignore step 6.
Instead, drag with
the mouse in the
Nib shape box:

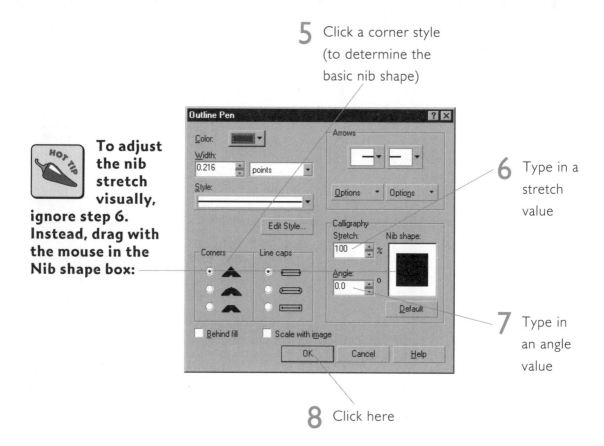

6 Type in a
stretch
value

7 Type in
an angle
value

8 Click here

Examples:

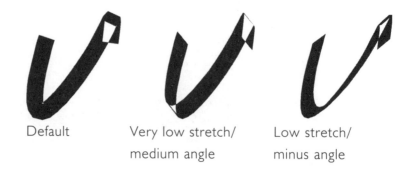

Default   Very low stretch/   Low stretch/
                 medium angle   minus angle

Further outline options

To launch the Outline Pen dialog, follow step 1 on page 85.

The Behind Fill option is specially useful for work with text outlines.

There are two additional outline options which are only accessible from within the Outline Pen dialog. Both can have a substantial impact on the efficiency of your outlines.

The Behind Fill option

Click this to have your outline placed behind an object's fill. This helps to adjust an outline which is too emphatic by making only half its thickness visible.

Behind Fill not active

Behind Fill in action

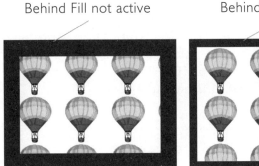

The Scale With Image option

This option ensures that outlines you apply are scaled proportionately when you resize an object.

The original resized by 200%, not using Scale With Image

The original resized using Scale With Image

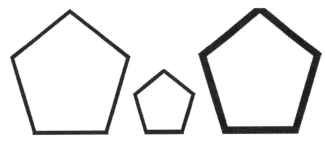

The original polygon

Setting outline defaults

By default, CorelDRAW applies the following outline defaults whenever you create a new graphic object:

- Width – around 0.2 points

- Colour – black

- No arrows, corners, line caps or calligraphic effects are in force

If you implement any of the processes we've discussed in this chapter *without pre-selecting an existing object*, CorelDRAW assumes you want to set revised default values for *all* future outlines (except text unless you specify this – see the HOT TIP). This is a useful device: it can save you a lot of time and effort.

 Before you carry out step 1 here, ensure that no objects are selected.

| Follow step 1 on page 85, then click this icon: in the Outline fly-out

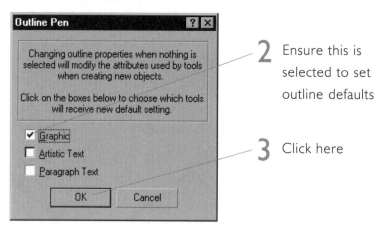

Re step 2 – select Artistic Text and/ or Paragraph Text if you want your new outline defaults to apply to these object types.

2 Ensure this is selected to set outline defaults

3 Click here

4 The Outline Pen dialog launches – set the appropriate outline defaults, then click OK

Henceforth, the outlines of any objects you create (in this and subsequent CorelDRAW sessions) will automatically attract these default values.

The Fill Tool

In this chapter, you'll discover how to fill CorelDRAW objects. You'll learn to use the five basic fill types. We'll also discuss how to copy fills between objects, easily and conveniently, and how to preset fill defaults for objects you create in all future editing sessions. Additionally, you'll learn how to apply (and tile) fills *interactively,* with the mouse, and also how to customise them even further with mesh fills.

Covers

Chapter Seven

An overview

Fills are probably one of CorelDRAW's most popular and useful features. Any closed object in CorelDRAW can be filled.

You can apply any of the following fill types:

- uniform fills

- pattern fills

- fountain fills

- texture fills

- PostScript fills

The permutations for each of these are almost infinite.

You can also apply fills on-the-fly, with the use of the mouse. When you've done so, you can further customise them by imposing a mesh (grid) and manipulating this.

You can fill objects by using (variously):

- the Color docker

- the various Fill dialogs

- on-screen colour palettes

The dialogs you can use offer the most precision, and change according to the function. For example, if you're imposing a fountain fill, you can work from the Fountain Fill dialog. Standard fills can be manipulated from within the Color docker.

General guidelines

Unlike outlines, there is no all-purpose dialog from which all fill settings can be implemented (there are too many of them). Instead, CorelDRAW provides a series of independent dialogs and the Color docker. The advantage of the docker (and colour palettes) is that they can be kept on-screen while you work with multiple fills.

CorelDRAW lets you copy fills from one object to another very easily and painlessly. Use this technique to save yourself a lot of time and effort.

...cont'd

You can use a shortcut to apply fills – the Eyedropper and Paintbucket tools.

Do the following in the Toolbox:

Click here

Move the mouse pointer to the correct location in a filled object. Left-click once – the selected fill is memorised. Now do the following in the Toolbox:

2 Click here

Click inside an empty, closed object; CorelDRAW inserts the copied fill.

Another labour-saving technique is the ability to preset fill defaults. By using this, you can ensure that any objects you create, in the current and any subsequent CorelDRAW editing session, automatically inherit the fill you've stipulated.

The illustration below shows a light-hearted use of the fill techniques we'll go on to discuss in the rest of this chapter:

A two-colour fill

A full-colour pattern fill

A bitmap pattern fill

A fountain (conical) fill

A texture (fractal) fill

Applying uniform fills

Uniform fills are solid, single-colour/shade fills. These are the easiest to impose, and arguably the most often used. You can apply uniform fills in two principal ways:

For how to create default fill properties (so that new objects automatically inherit them), see page 134.

- by using on-screen colour palettes

- by using the Color docker

The Color docker provides the most complexity; use this to achieve greater fill precision.

In addition, you can use the Fill fly-out to *remove* fills directly. (We'll look at the use of on-screen palettes and the Color docker on pages 113–114.)

Removing existing fills

First, select the closed object(s) whose fill you want to remove. Now turn to the Toolbox and carry out the following steps, as appropriate:

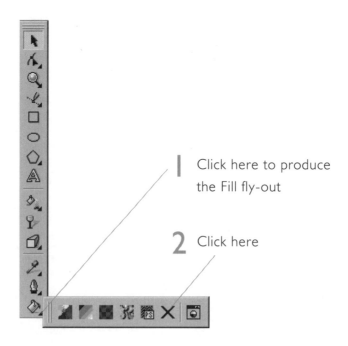

1 Click here to produce the Fill fly-out

2 Click here

...cont'd

By default, colour palettes display on the right of the screen.

To reposition a palette, click it outside the colour swatches, then drag it to another screen edge.

If no colour palette is currently visible, pull down the Window menu and click Color Palettes. In the sub-menu, choose the palette you want to use.

(You can have more than one open at a time.)

Click here: to expand the active colour palette so more colours are visible.

(To shrink it, click anywhere outside the palette.)

There are two ways to apply *customised* uniform fills:

Using colour palettes

First select one or more objects you want to fill. Then refer to the on-screen palette – see page 9 if you're not sure of its location, and see the HOT TIP if it isn't currently on screen.

Carry out the following procedure:

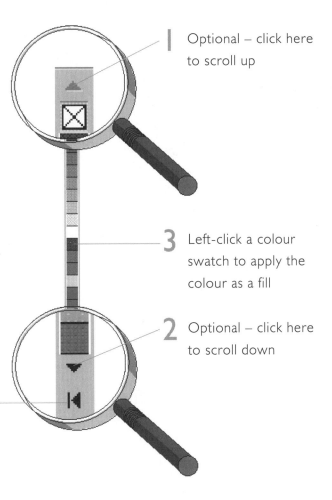

1   Optional – click here to scroll up

3   Left-click a colour swatch to apply the colour as a fill

2   Optional – click here to scroll down

Using the Color docker

Carry out the following steps:

1 Activate the Pick Tool in the on-screen Toolbox

2 Select the object(s) you want to fill

3 Follow step 1 on page 112

4 Click here

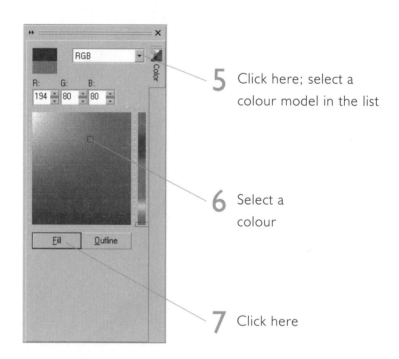

5 Click here; select a colour model in the list

6 Select a colour

7 Click here

Pattern fills – an overview

Pattern fills are special fills where one symmetrical design is repeated to occupy the available space (CorelDRAW calls this process 'tiling') without any perceptible seams. You can use three basic pattern types:

- Two-colour patterns
- Full-colour patterns
- Bitmaps

Two-colour patterns are particularly simple designs (by default, black and white) which are easy and quick to use, though nonetheless effective.

Full-colour patterns are more complex, with greater colour detail.

Bitmaps are photograph-quality designs which can place heavy demands on your system in terms of memory use. However, they do provide excellent results.

Examples:

A pre-defined two-colour pattern

A pre-defined full-colour pattern

A pre-defined bitmap pattern

Using two-colour pattern fills

You apply 2-colour fills from within a special dialog.

1 Activate the Pick Tool in the on-screen Toolbox

2 Select the object(s) you want to fill

3 Follow step 1 on page 112

4 Click here

Re step 7 – to specify the foreground fill colour, click Front. In the list, select a colour.
 To specify the background colour, click Back. In the list, select a colour.

5 Ensure 2-color is selected

6 Click here; select a 2-colour pattern in the list

You can also skew and/or rotate 2-colour fills. Simply type the relevant values (as degrees) into the Skew or Rotate fields before you carry out step 9.

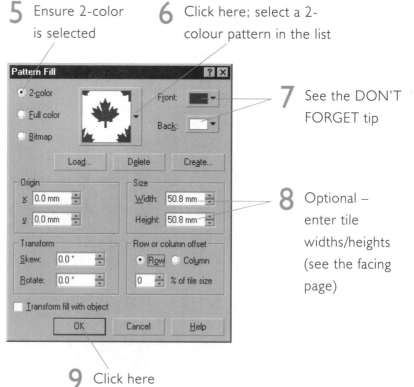

7 See the DON'T FORGET tip

8 Optional – enter tile widths/heights (see the facing page)

9 Click here

...cont'd

 You can also customise tile width and height on-the-fly, with the mouse – see page 130.

2-colour fills in action

When you apply a 2-colour pattern, you can customise the tile width and height – see step 8 on the facing page. Doing this can have a dramatic effect on the overall pattern.

The illustration below shows a standard 2-colour fill with the default width/height settings:

Width — 50.8 mm

Height — 50.8 mm

The next illustration shows the effect of increasing these to:

Width — 100 mm

Height — 100 mm

Using full-colour pattern fills

You apply full-colour fills from within a special dialog.

1 Activate the Pick Tool in the on-screen Toolbox

2 Select the object(s) you want to fill

3 Follow step 1 on page 112

4 Click here

5 Ensure Full color is selected

6 Click here; select a full-colour pattern in the list

You can also skew and/or rotate full-colour fills. Simply type the relevant values (as degrees) into the Skew or Rotate fields before you carry out step 8.

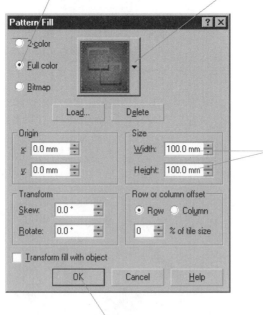

7 Optional – enter tile widths/heights (see the facing page)

8 Click here

...cont'd

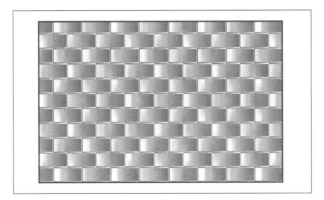

You can also customise tile width and height on-the-fly, with the mouse – see page 130.

Full-colour fills in action

When you apply a full-colour pattern, you can customise the tile width/height – see step 7 on the facing page. Doing this can have a dramatic effect on the overall pattern.

The illustration below shows a standard full-colour fill with the default width/height settings:

Width — 50.8 mm

Height — 50.8 mm

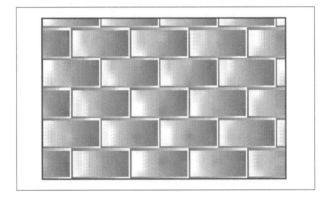

The next illustration shows the effect of decreasing these to:

Width — 25 mm

Height — 25 mm

Using bitmap pattern fills

You apply bitmap pattern fills from within a special dialog.

1 Activate the Pick Tool in the on-screen Toolbox

2 Select the object(s) you want to fill

3 Follow step 1 on page 112

4 Click here

5 Ensure Bitmap is selected   6 Click here; select a bitmap pattern in the list

You can also skew and/or rotate bitmap fills. Simply type the relevant values (as degrees) into the Skew or Rotate fields before you carry out step 8.

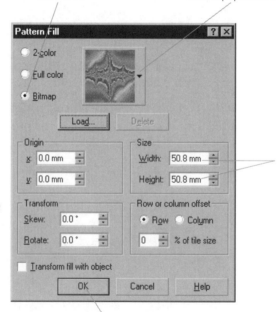

7 Optional – enter tile widths/heights (see the facing page)

8 Click here

...cont'd

You can also customise tile width and height on-the-fly, with the mouse – see page 130.

Bitmap fills in action

When you apply a bitmap pattern, you can customise the tile width and height – see step 7 on the facing page. Doing this can have a dramatic effect on the overall pattern.

The illustration below shows a standard bitmap fill with the default width/height settings:

Width — 50.8 mm

Height — 50.8 mm

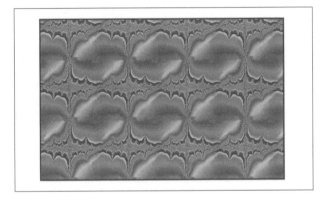

The next illustration shows the effect of amending these to:

Width — 100 mm

Height — 10 mm

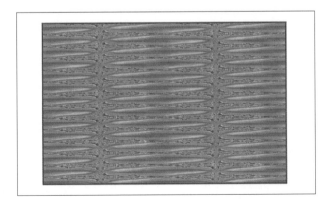

Using fountain fills

Fountain fills – also known as gradient fills – are fills which involve a gradual transition from one colour to another via a series of steps. You can specify:

- the two colours

- where the transition should start

- how gradual the transition should be (i.e. the number of steps)

There are four kinds of fountain fills:

Linear	Radial	Conical	Square

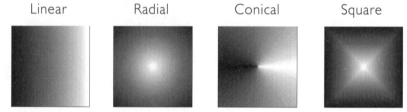

Applying fountain fills

1 Activate the Pick Tool in the on-screen Toolbox

2 Select the object(s) you want to fill

3 Follow step 1 on page 112

4 Click here

...cont'd

As a shortcut, instead of following steps 5–9, click the arrow button to the right of the Presets field and choose from a wide selection of pre-defined fountain fills.

Then follow step 10.

Re step 6 – by default, fountain fills are defined in 256 steps.

5 Click here; select a fountain fill type

6 Optional – click ▣ then type in the no. of steps

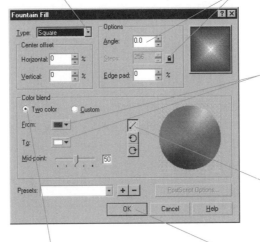

8 Click either or both colour buttons; select the colour you want from the list

9 Ensure this is active

7 Make sure this is selected

10 Click here

Example

The illustration below shows a preset fill called Gold Plated:

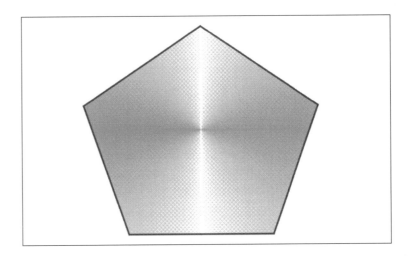

Using texture fills

Texture fills are fractal-based, which means they mimic natural materials very realistically. In CorelDRAW, texture fills are organised into seven texture libraries:

- Samples

- Samples 5

- Samples 6

- Samples 7

- Samples 8

- Samples 9

- Styles

You should apply texture fills with discretion. Though spectacular – not to say highly enjoyable! – they're very memory intensive. They also take up a lot of hard disk space, and can occasionally cause problems when printed.

The illustration below shows one of CorelDRAW's texture fills:

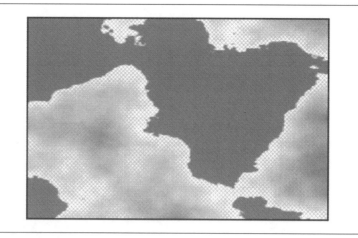

One feature of texture fills is that they're almost infinitely customisable; each texture offers millions of control permutations.

...cont'd

Applying texture fills

1 Activate the Pick Tool in the on-screen Toolbox

2 Select the object(s) you want to fill

3 Follow step 1 on page 112

4 Click here

If you change the texture settings, click the Preview button at any time to see what the new texture looks like before you carry out step 9.

5 Click here; select a texture library from the drop-down list

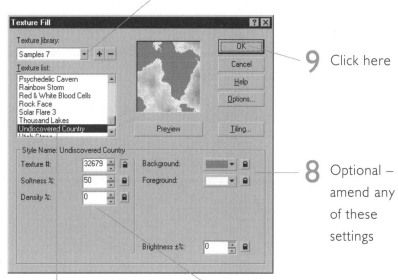

9 Click here

8 Optional – amend any of these settings

To re-tile texture fills, click the Tiling button. Complete the Width: and Height: fields, then click OK.

The number and type of fields present in the lower half of the dialog depend on which texture you choose in step 6.

6 Click the texture you want to apply

7 Optional – amend any of these settings

Using interactive fills

You can use a special tool to apply any of the fills we've discussed in this chapter *interactively*. This means that you can adjust any of the fill parameters on-screen, with the help of the mouse and Property Bar.

Creating a fill interactively

1 Activate the Pick Tool in the on-screen Toolbox

2 Select the object you want to fill

3 Refer to the Toolbox and perform the following additional steps:

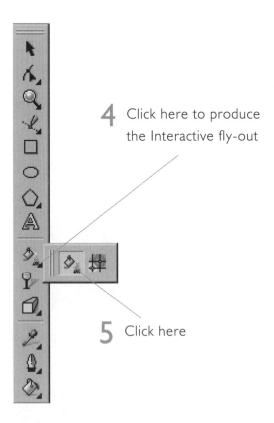

4 Click here to produce the Interactive fly-out

5 Click here

...cont'd

Re step 6 – the Property Bar changes according to which fill type is chosen.

After step 6, complete more fields in the Property Bar, as appropriate.
  For instance, clicking any of these fields:

selects a specific fountain fill type, while these:

specify the pattern fill type.

6 Click here in the Property Bar; in the list, select a fill type

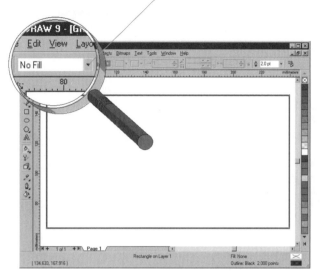

CorelDRAW fills the object. Do any of the following:

7 Drag anywhere in the object to redefine the fill

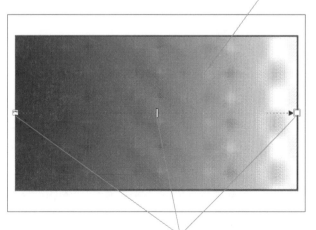

8 Drag any of these to redefine the fill

Creating mesh fills

You can use a special implementation of the Interactive tool – the Mesh Fill tool – to customise fills you've already applied in entirely unique ways. Like the interactive fills we discussed on pages 126–127, you can adjust mesh fills interactively, with the help of the mouse and Property Bar.

When you create a mesh fill, you're actually applying an interactive grid, complete with nodes. By dragging:

- **the grid structure**
- **any of the nodes**

you can redefine the underlying fill in spectacular ways.

  You can also add your own nodes, for even greater effect.

Creating mesh fills

1 Apply a fill to the relevant object, using any of the techniques discussed on pages 112–125

2 Refer to the Toolbox and perform the following additional steps:

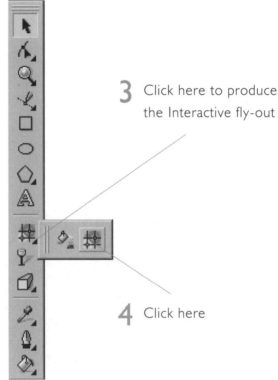

3 Click here to produce the Interactive fly-out

4 Click here

...cont'd

5 Click the filled object

6 Specify the no. of horizontal/vertical columns

7 Drag the mesh or a node

 Clicking a node also reveals other nodes:

Nodes

To add your own nodes, ensure the Mesh Fill tool is active. Then click anywhere on the mesh.

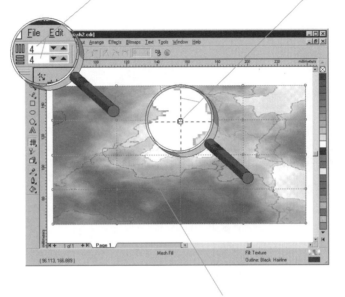

CorelDRAW applies an interactive mesh

Example:

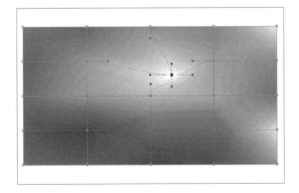

The end result of dragging the node flagged in the higher illustration

Tiling fills interactively

We've already discussed (see pages 117, 119, 121 and 125) how to adjust fill tiling by using the respective Fill dialogs. However, you can also use the Interactive Fill tool to specify tiling dimensions on-the-fly.

This is a dynamic technique (the screen updates automatically as you make a change) which makes tiling both easy and fun.

Specifying tiling interactively

Refer to the Toolbox and perform the following steps:

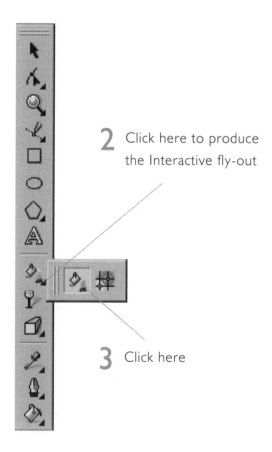

2 Click here to produce the Interactive fly-out

3 Click here

...cont'd

4 Click any object to which a 2-colour, full-colour, bitmap or texture fill has been applied

If the interactive tiling controls aren't where you want them, simply click elsewhere in the fill before you carry out step 5.

5 Drag any of these to re-tile the fill

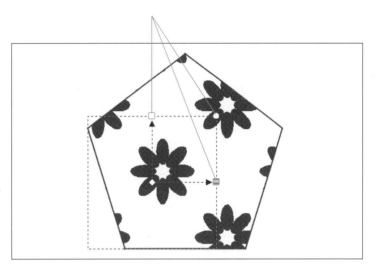

Re step 5 – interactive tiling is so useful because you can see results immediately, and decide if they're suitable. If they're not, a new tiling configuration is only a couple of mouse clicks away.

Example:

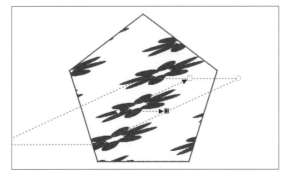

The upper middle handle has been dragged to the right

Using PostScript fills

You can also use PostScript fills if you have a GDI printer (e.g. an inkjet optimised for use with Microsoft Windows) installed.

If you have a PostScript printer installed, you have access to a range of additional fills. However, you should bear in mind the following:

- some PostScript fills are complex and require a lot of time to draw or print, so they should be used with discretion

- PostScript fills do not display faithfully on-screen (what you see is a low-quality, informational header)

- you have to use a special dialog to apply PostScript fills

Creating PostScript fills

1 Activate the Pick Tool in the on-screen Toolbox

2 Select the object(s) you want to fill

3 Follow step 1 on page 112

4 Click here

5 Click a fill

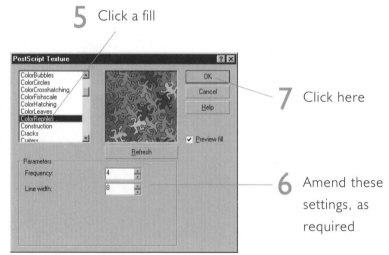

If you want to know what PostScript fills look like before you apply them, make sure Preview fill is selected (as here).

7 Click here

6 Amend these settings, as required

Copying fills

There is a simple technique you can use to copy any kind of fill from one object to another. This saves time and energy: you don't have to go to the trouble of noting a fill's characteristics and then applying these laboriously to the second object.

1 Activate the Pick Tool in the Toolbox and select the object you want to fill

2 Follow steps 4–5 on page 126

3 Refer to the Property Bar and do the following:

Here, the Property Bar is shown as an independent toolbar. On your screen, however, it may be docked.

4 Click here

5 Position the Copy Fill cursor on or in the object to be copied; left-click once

After step 5, the selected fill is copied into the empty object.

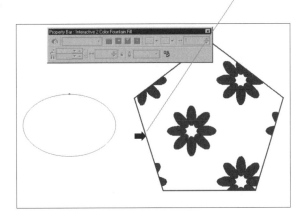

Setting fill defaults

By default, CorelDRAW applies no fill whenever you create a new graphic object. However, you can change this if you want. You can have CorelDRAW automatically impose any fill you opt for as standard.

If you implement any of the processes we've discussed in this chapter *without pre-selecting an existing object*, CorelDRAW assumes you want to set revised default values for *all* future outlines (except text unless you specify this – see the HOT TIP). This is a useful device: it can save you a lot of time and effort.

Before you carry out step 1, ensure that no objects are selected.

Follow step 1 on page 112, then click any of these icons in the Fill fly-out:

Re step 2 – select Artistic Text and/ or Paragraph Text if you want your new fill defaults to apply to these object types.

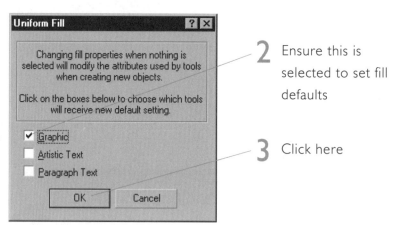

2 Ensure this is selected to set fill defaults

3 Click here

4 Complete the dialog which launches, then click OK

Henceforth, the fills of any objects you create (in this and subsequent CorelDRAW sessions) will automatically attract these default values.

The Artistic Media Tool

In this chapter, you'll learn how to use the Artistic Media Tool to create specialist curves, complete with artistic effects. You'll create curves with preset shapes, and with pre-defined brushes; then you'll go on to create your own brushes from imported text or graphics, and use these to generate customised curves. Finally, you'll draw curves by spraying objects onto the Drawing Window, and create curves which mimic calligraphic effects.

Covers

Chapter Eight

Using Preset mode

The Artistic Media Tool has various modes. The main ones are:

- **Preset – produces curves with differing shapes**
- **Brush – applies text or shapes to curves**
- **Object Sprayer – draws curves with images**
- **Calligraphic – mimics calligraphic effects**

You can use the Artistic Media Tool to create curves with a variety of artistic effects – see the DON'T FORGET tip.

Drawing with Preset mode

1 Carry out step 1 on page 40

2 Click here, then refer to the Property Bar:

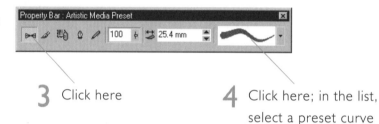

3 Click here

4 Click here; in the list, select a preset curve

5 Click where you want the curve to start, then hold down the mouse button and drag. Release the button

Preset mode in action:

You can also use the Property Bar to adjust the curve in these ways:

Specify the amount of smoothing (in the range: 0–100)

25.4 mm

Type in a curve width

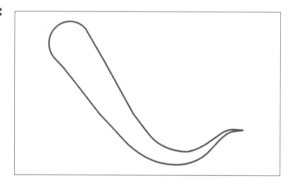

A simple preset curve

Using Brush mode

To create a new brush based on an object, import it into the active document and select it. Follow steps 1–3. Click this button on the Property Bar:

In the Save As dialog, name the new brush, then click Save.
Now follow step 5.

Brush mode lets you apply a preset brush, or a pre-saved graphic/text object.

Drawing with Brush mode

1 Carry out step 1 on page 40

2 Click here, then refer to the Property Bar:

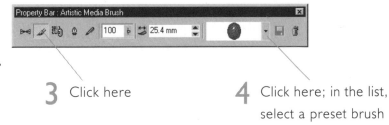

3 Click here

4 Click here; in the list, select a preset brush

You can also use the Property Bar to adjust the curve in these ways:

Specify the amount of smoothing (in the range: 0–100)

Type in a curve width

5 Click where you want the curve to start, then hold down the mouse button and drag. Release the button

Brush mode in action:

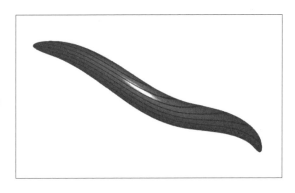

A sample preset brush curve

Using Object Sprayer mode

To draw with Calligraphic mode, follow steps 1–2. In step 3, click this button:

Omit step 4. Instead, follow the instructions in the HOT TIP on page 137. Finally, carry out step 5.

A simple calligraphic curve is shown below:

You can use the Object Sprayer to spray objects along a curve.

Spraying objects

| 1 Carry out step 1 on page 40

2 Click here, then refer to the Property Bar:

3 Click here   4 Click here; in the list, select a preset spray

5 Click where you want the curve to start, then hold down the mouse button and drag. Release the button

Brush mode in action:

You can also use the Property Bar to adjust the curve in this way:

Specify the amount of smoothing (in the range: 0–100)

A sample preset brush curve

The Interactive Tools

In this chapter, you'll learn how to use CorelDRAW's Interactive tools which allow you to perform complex reshaping and design operations on objects visually, with the mouse. You'll warp objects; apply interactive extrusions and blends; apply interactive envelopes; and then use free transformations. Finally, you'll contour objects and apply drop shadows, both interactively.

Covers

Chapter Nine

Interactivity – an overview

We've already looked at the following aspects of the use of interactive tools:

- the Interactive Fill tool (see page 126–127)

- the interactive Mesh Fill tool (see pages 128–129)

- interactive fill tiling (see page 130)

However, CorelDRAW offers the following additional interactive tools:

- the Interactive Distortion tool

- the Interactive Extrude tool

- the Interactive Blend tool

- the Interactive Envelope tool

- the Free Transformation tools

- the Interactive Drop Shadow tool

- the Interactive Contour tool

In any of the interactive tools, you can use the Property Bar to specify additional settings which are not discussed separately.

For example, when you use the Interactive Drop Shadow tool, you can specify:
- **shadow feathering**
- **shadow opacity**
- **horizontal/ vertical shadow offsets**
- **shadow direction**
- **shadow colour**

These allow you to reshape or reconfigure objects on-the-fly, with the mouse. As you do this, CorelDRAW displays a dashed version of the changes you're making, so you can preview what they'll look like once they're implemented.

Some of the interactive tools relate to (and improve on) functions which already exist in CorelDRAW. For instance, you can rotate objects with the techniques discussed on page 49. However, if you do so with the Free Rotation tool discussed on page 145, the process is much more customisable – see the HOT TIP.

Artistic text which has been shadowed

Distorting objects

You can apply interactive distortions to objects, using the mouse.

You can distort any object, including artistic (but not paragraph) text.

Distorting on-the-fly
Do the following in the Toolbox:

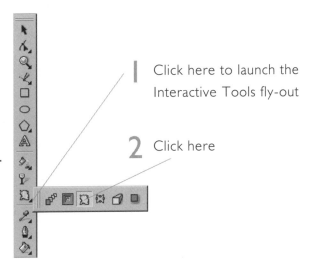

I Click here to launch the Interactive Tools fly-out

2 Click here

Re step 3 – you can carry out three types of distortion:
- **Push and Pull**
- **Zipper**
- **Twister**

The best way to become familiar with the effects they produce is to use them.

Now perform the following operations:

3 In the Property Bar, select a distortion type

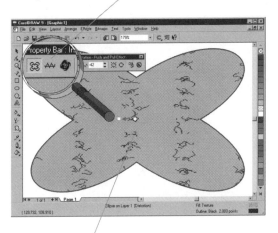

Here, an ellipse has been subjected to Push and Pull distortion

Don't be afraid to apply multiple distortion effects e.g. apply Push and Pull and Zipper to the same object.

4 Drag appropriately to define the distortion

Extruding objects

Before you carry out step 3, do the following in the Property Bar:

Ensure this is active

After step 3, drag this symbol in the extrusion:

to alter the depth e.g:

You can apply interactive extrusions to objects, using the mouse.

Extruding on-the-fly

Refer to the Toolbox, then carry out the following steps:

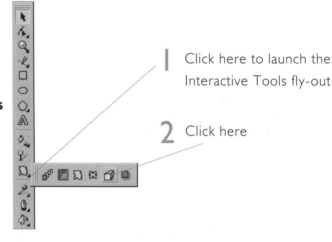

1 Click here to launch the Interactive Tools fly-out

2 Click here

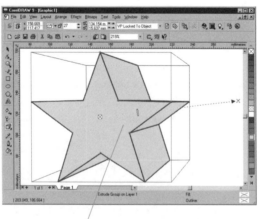

Here, a star has been extruded to the right

After step 3, alter the extrusion direction by dragging this marker:

X

3 Click anywhere in the object and drag to define the extrusion

4 Click the Pick Tool in the Toolbox

Blending objects

You can contour objects interactively.

You can blend objects interactively, using the mouse.

Blending on-the-fly
Refer to the Toolbox, then carry out the following steps:

Select an object with the Pick Tool. Follow step 1; in step 2, though, click this icon instead:

Drag in or out over the object to define contours.

Once defined, contours can be recoloured via these buttons in the Property Bar:

Outline colour

Fill colour

In this instance, the final blend looks like this:

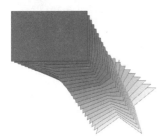

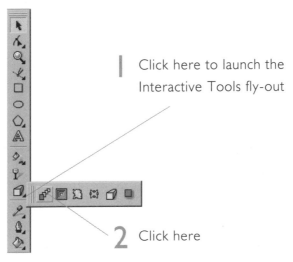

1 Click here to launch the Interactive Tools fly-out

2 Click here

Here, a star is being blended with a rectangle

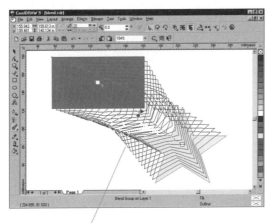

3 Drag from one object to another to define the blend

4 Click the Pick Tool in the Toolbox

Interactive envelopes

Step 3 positions an envelope (of exactly the same dimensions) around the relevant object.

You can reshape objects by applying an envelope and manipulating this interactively, using the mouse.

Using interactive envelopes

Refer to the Toolbox and carry out the following steps:

Re step 4 – you can carry out four types of envelope reshaping:

• **Straight Line**
• **Single Arc**
• **Double Arc**
• **Unconstrained (the default)**

The best way to become familiar with the effects they produce is to use them.

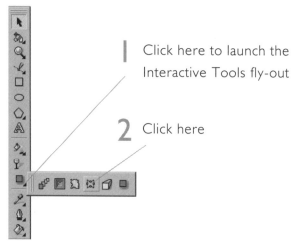

1 Click here to launch the Interactive Tools fly-out

2 Click here

3 Click the object you want to reshape

4 In the Property Bar, select one of these

In this instance, the final result may look like this:

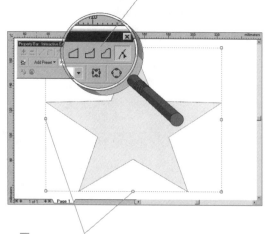

Here, a star has been reshaped by dragging its envelope to the right

5 Drag any node to reshape the underlying object

Free transformations

You can apply a variety of interactive transformations.

Before you carry out step 1, use the Pick Tool to select the object you want to transform.

Transforming on-the-fly
Do the following in the Toolbox:

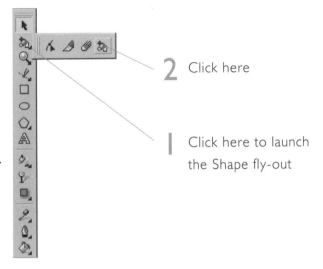

2 Click here

| Click here to launch the Shape fly-out

Re step 3 – you can carry out four types of interactive transformation:

- **Free Rotation – rotates an object around a rotation centre**
- **Free Angle Reflection – mirrors objects**
- **Free Scale – scales objects along the horizontal/ vertical axes**
- **Free Skew – slants an object's horizontal/ vertical lines**

Now perform the following operations:

3 In the Property Bar, select a transformation type

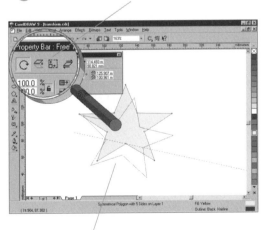

Here, a Free Rotation operation is being carried out

4 Click to create an anchor point, then drag to transform the object

Interactive shadows

You can apply drop shadows to objects, interactively.

Shadowing on-the-fly

Refer to the Toolbox, then carry out the following steps:

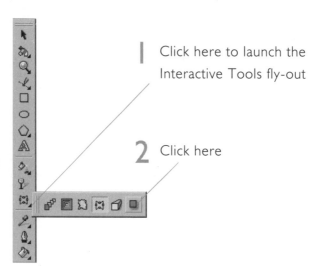

1 Click here to launch the Interactive Tools fly-out

2 Click here

To change the shadow colour, do the following in the Property Bar:

Click here; in the list, select a colour

3 Click the object you want to shadow

Re step 4 – dragging objects to the side produces a 3-D shadow effect.

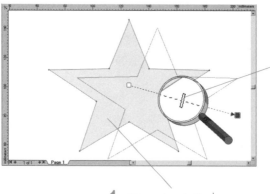

Optional – drag this to adjust the shadow's opacity

In this instance, the final result may look like this:

4 Drag to define a drop shadow

5 Release the mouse button, then click the Pick Tool in the Toolbox

Working with images

In this chapter, you'll learn how to import bitmap and vector images into CorelDRAW, via a dialog and the Scrapbook (you'll also use this to import clip art from the Internet). You'll learn something about the various graphics formats, and also how to perform operations which are specific to bitmaps (including applying special effects). Finally, you'll make your image work easier and more convenient with colour styles, and export your work into third-party formats.

Covers

Chapter Ten

An overview

Be careful how you resize imported bitmaps: rescaling them can cause distortion. If you must resize bitmaps, do so in round numbers if possible – i.e. use increments or decrements of 50%, 100%, 150% etc.

You can insert graphics directly into artistic or paragraph text. (When you do so, CorelDRAW treats them as text characters.)
   First, select the image you want to embed. Press Ctrl+X (this deletes the graphic and copies it to the Windows Clipboard). Select the Text tool in the Toolbox; click in the text where you want the graphic to appear. Press Shift+Insert.

CorelDRAW works with both bitmap and vector images. We touched on this briefly in Chapter 7; however, we now need to go into the subject in rather more detail.

Bitmap images

Bitmaps consist of pixels (dots) arranged in such a way that they form a graphic image. Because of the very nature of bitmaps, the question of 'resolution' – the sharpness of an image expressed in dpi (dots per inch) – is very important. Bitmaps look best if they're displayed at their correct resolution. CorelDRAW imports (i.e. translates into its own format) a wide variety of third-party bitmap formats.

Look at the illustration below.

This image – one of the many royalty free-images supplied by Corel Corporation – was imported into CorelDRAW in a matter of seconds.

Once you've imported a bitmap into CorelDRAW, you can:

- colour black and white bitmaps
- crop bitmaps
- rescale bitmaps
- rotate or skew bitmaps
- apply special effects

Once you've finished working with bitmaps in CorelDRAW, you can export the finished result as another bitmap, or as a vector image. In this way, they can be utilised in other programs which are unable to import CorelDRAW's native .CDR or .CMX formats.

Vector images

CorelDRAW will also import vector graphics files in formats native to other programs. Vector images consist of, and are defined by, algebraic equations. One practical result of this is that they can be rescaled without any loss of definition. Another corollary is that they're not as complex as bitmaps since they contain less detail.

The illustration below is one of the images supplied with CorelDRAW. These images are supplied in .CDR format.

 Vector images can also include bitmap information. For example, PostScript files often have a low-quality, illustrative header (used for preview purposes) which is a bitmap.

Once you've imported a vector image into CorelDRAW, you can edit it in much the same way as you edit objects you've created yourself. (See Chapters 2 and 3 for more information.)

When finished, vector images can also be exported, either as vector or bitmap files.

Brief notes on image formats

CorelDRAW will happily import/export a wide selection of bitmap and vector graphic formats. These are some of the main formats:

Bitmap formats

Many bitmap formats have compression as an option. This allows bitmaps – often very large – to be stored on disk in much smaller files.

PCX   An old standby. Originated with PC Paintbrush, a paint program. Used for years to transfer graphics data between Windows applications. Supports compression.

TIFF   Tagged Image File Format. Suffix: .TIF. If anything, even more widely used than PCX, across a whole range of platforms and applications. Supports numerous types and levels of compression.

BMP   Not as common as PCX and TIFF, but still popular. One drawback: sometimes, compression isn't available. It is, however, with CorelDRAW.

TGA   Targa. A high-end format, and also a bridge with so-called low-end computers (e.g. Amiga and Atari). Often used in PC and Mac paint and ray-tracing programs because of its high-resolution colour fidelity. Supports compression.

GIF   Graphics Interchange Format. Developed for the on-line transmission of graphics data across the CompuServe network. Just about any Windows program – and a lot more besides – will read GIF. Disadvantage: it can't handle more than 256 colours. One of the few graphics formats which can be used in HTML (HyperText Markup Language) documents on the World Wide Web. Compression is supported.

PCD   (Kodak) PhotoCD. Used primarily to store photographs on CD. Corel Corporation sells a vast range of images in this format.

JPEG   Joint Photographic Experts Group. Suffix: .JPG. Used on the PC and Mac for the storage and display of photographs. One of the few graphics formats which can be used in HTML (HyperText Markup Language) documents on the World Wide Web. A very high level of compression is built into the format.

> **You can use standard Windows techniques to copy, cut and paste graphics/objects into CorelDRAW documents. However, you can also:**
>
> • **'duplicate' objects. Select one or more objects; press Ctrl+D. CorelDRAW inserts an identical copy, but at a precise horizontal/ vertical offset**
>
> • **'clone' objects. Select one or more objects; pull down the Edit menu and click Clone. CorelDRAW inserts an identical copy. However, any changes you make to the original (the 'master') are automatically applied to the clone(s)**

Vector formats

CGM   Computer Graphics Metafile. Frequently used in the past, especially as a medium for clip-art transmission. Less frequently used nowadays.

EPS   Encapsulated PostScript. Perhaps the most widely used PostScript format. Actually, PostScript (a programming language in its own right) combines vector *and* bitmap data very successfully. Incorporates a low-resolution bitmap 'header' for preview purposes. If you want to export to a vector format and have a choice, you'd be well advised to use EPS.

WMF   Windows Metafile. Similar to CGM, but even more frequently used. Used for information exchange between just about all Windows programs. Often produces files which are much smaller than the equivalent bitmaps (though not because of compression – there isn't any). If you need a vector format and can't use EPS, use WMF wherever possible.

AI   A special implementation of the PostScript format, native to Adobe Illustrator. A frequently used standard.

Importing images

You can import both bitmap and vector images into CorelDRAW very easily and quickly.

 If you haven't already done so, press Ctrl+N (before you carry out step 1) to create a new, blank document to host the image.

1 Pull down the File menu and click Import

3 Click here; in the list, click the drive which hosts the graphic file

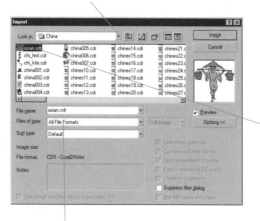

 If you want to view an image before you import it (as here), make sure Preview is ticked.

4 Double-click a picture entry

 Re step 4 – you may have to double-click one or more folders first, to locate the image you want to open.

2 Make sure All File Formats is shown. If it isn't, click the arrow and select it from the list

5 CorelDRAW displays a customised mouse pointer: Position this where you want the picture inserted and left-click once

 If, when you try to import an image, CorelDRAW fails to recognise it, the relevant filter may not be present.
  To rectify this, rerun Setup.

An inserted image

Using the Scrapbook

If you haven't already done so, press Ctrl+N (before you carry out step 1) to create a new, blank document to host the image(s).

If you want, you can connect to FTP sites.

With your Internet connection live, click Scrapbook, Ftp Sites in the Tools menu. Right-click in the Scrapbook; click Go To Site in the menu. In the dialog, type an address e.g: ftp.corel.com Click OK. Follow steps 1–3.

To insert a photo, click Scrapbook, Photos in the Tools menu. When requested, make sure the relevant CD is in the drive. Follow steps 1–3.

You can also import images via the Scrapbook. The Scrapbook is a docker window from which you can drag pictures into your CorelDRAW documents.

Adding images from the Scrapbook

Ensure the relevant CD is in the drive. Pull down the Tools menu and click Scrapbook, Clipart. Now do the following:

1 Double-click the relevant folder(s) until the Scrapbook displays image icons

2 Click an icon

3 Drag the icon into your document and release the mouse button

Colouring a black and white bitmap

It's sometimes useful to work with monochrome bitmaps –
you can add background/foreground colours to them:

1 Select the relevant black and white bitmap

2 Refer to the colour palette(s) on the right of the screen and
do the following:

If no colour palette is currently visible, pull down the Window menu and click Color Palettes. In the sub-menu, choose the palette you want to use.
(You can have more than one open at a time.)

3 Optional – click here
to scroll up

5 Left-click a colour swatch to
apply the colour as a
background, or right-click it to
apply it as a foreground

4 Optional – click here
to scroll down

Click here: to expand the active colour palette so more colours are visible.
(To shrink it, click anywhere outside the palette.)

A mono
image has had
foreground &
background
colours
applied

Tracing bitmaps

 If you find the tracing process doesn't work well, you need to run CorelTRACE, a separate Corel program.

While vector images consist of objects which can be isolated and acted on, bitmaps don't (pixels can't be classified in the same way). One attribute a pixel can possess, however, is colour. This means you *can* identify bitmap components; CorelDRAW calls this 'tracing'. When you trace part of a bitmap, you isolate pixels of the same colour, and can then apply standard outline/fill techniques.

Tracing a bitmap

First, use the Pick Tool to select the relevant bitmap. Then refer to the Toolbox and carry out the following steps:

 Tracing will only work if you've pre-selected a bitmap. If you haven't, CorelDRAW assumes you want to draw a freehand line or curve.

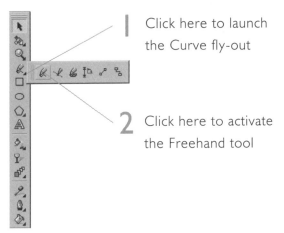

1 Click here to launch the Curve fly-out

2 Click here to activate the Freehand tool

3 The cursor becomes: ⊣── Move this over the section of the bitmap which you want to trace, then left-click once

4 Apply the appropriate outline and/or fill

Here, a traced bitmap section has had a texture fill applied

Cropping bitmaps

One thing you can't do is mark out a section of a bitmap and then extract it as an image in its own right.

In CorelDRAW, cropping is the process whereby you shrink a bitmap's apparent outline, so that less of the image is visible. Although a cropped bitmap only displays that part of it which lies within the new outline, the image data outside the outline is still there; it's simply hidden.

Cropping a bitmap

Refer to the Toolbox, then carry out the following steps:

There are two corollaries to cropping:

- **because no data is actually removed, the file size is unaltered**
- **you can restore the original image, however many crop operations have been performed – simply press Ctrl+Z, or drag the node(s) back to their original location**

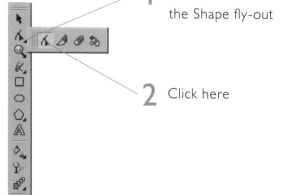

1 Click here to launch the Shape fly-out

2 Click here

3 Select the bitmap you want to crop

4 Drag in one or more of the visible nodes

Re step 4 – hold down Ctrl as you drag to ensure horizontal or vertical cropping.

The upper right corner of the bitmap has been cropped

Resizing & rotating/skewing images

Resizing

You can rescale both bitmap and vector images imported into CorelDRAW using standard Windows techniques. However, you should bear in mind that increasing or decreasing the size of bitmap images results in distortion, to varying degrees. To minimise this, you should do the following:

A certain amount of bitmap distortion is sometimes acceptable, especially with high-resolution images (16 million colours or over).

- try to achieve the correct resolution/size in the *originating* program, before you import the image into CorelDRAW

- only rescale within CorelDRAW (especially in the case of bitmaps) if you absolutely have to

- if you do have to, rescale wherever possible in increments or decrements which are whole numbers (e.g. 200%/ 300%/400%) – mathematically, this results in sharper images. Failing this, use 150%/250% etc.

Rotating/skewing

You can rotate or skew bitmaps in the same way that you can rotate or skew objects you create yourself. (See pages 45 and 145 for how to do this.)

Having said this, you should bear in mind the following tips:

Applying special effects to bitmaps (see page 158) is also a time-consuming process.

- Large, complex bitmaps can require a lot of processing power and time to rotate or skew. To help mitigate against this, follow the relevant instructions on pages 17–18 to enter Draft view mode. Broadly speaking, this forces bitmaps to display less accurately, but saves time. (Printing is unaffected.)

- Alternatively, follow the instructions on pages 17–18 to enter Wireframe or Simple Wireframe view modes. In both Wireframe modes, objects display as outlines (to a greater or less extent, depending on the number of colours your display is using), and screen redrawing is even quicker. The disadvantage is that Wireframe mode tends to reveal very little image detail. (Printing is unaffected.)

Bitmap special effects

You can apply lenses to objects. Create a closed object, then move it over the drawing you want to change. Press Alt+F3. Do the following in the Lens docker:

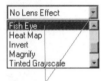

Click the arrow, then a lens

In the field(s) below this in the docker, specify the extent of the lens. Then click Apply. (The magnifying glasses in this book are examples of the Magnify lens.)

You can apply a large number of special effects to bitmaps within CorelDRAW. Examples include:

- 2D and 3D effects

- varieties of Blur, Noise and Sharpness

- Artistic and Colour Transformation effects

- an assortment of plug-ins (additional specialist programs)

Applying special effects

Select the bitmap(s). Pull down the Bitmaps menu and carry out the following steps:

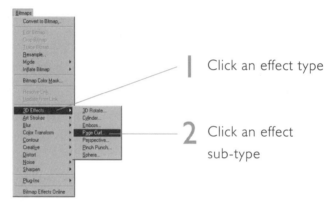

1 Click an effect type

2 Click an effect sub-type

3 Often, CorelDRAW launches a further dialog. Complete this as appropriate, then click OK

Re steps 1 and 2 – you can choose from a large number of effects (e.g. Stained Glass, Watercolour and Cubist) taken from Corel PHOTO-PAINT.

The 3D/Page Curl special effect in action

Colour styles

In Chapter 5, we looked at the use of text styles. You can also work with colour styles. You can create a colour style with the use of colour palettes, and then apply it to a drawing. Once a style has been applied, changing it also updates all objects on which the style has been imposed.

Creating a colour style

Pull down the Tools menu and click Color Styles. Now do the following:

Click an image entry in the docker

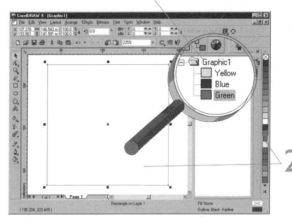

2 Drag a colour onto the selected graphic

Applying a colour style

Carry out the following:

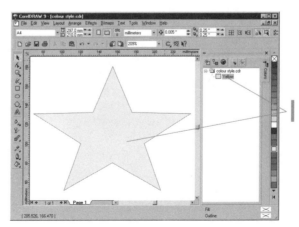

Drag a style onto the relevant object

Exporting images

When you've finished working with an imported graphics image, the normal – and correct – response is to save it as a CorelDRAW file. However, it's sometimes necessary to 'export' your work in a format which can be read into other programs. The problem is that few applications will read .CDR files directly. Even those that will are usually limited to earlier-version formats.

After step 4, double-click one or more folders (as appropriate) until you locate the correct one.

1 Consult the documentation which came with the program to find out which formats are supported

2 Pull down the File menu and click Export

4 Click here; in the drop-down list, click a drive

Re step 3 – if the format you want to export to isn't in the list, you may not have installed the required filter during installation. To rectify this, rerun Setup.

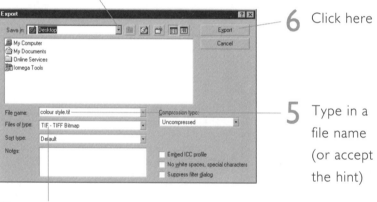

6 Click here

5 Type in a file name (or accept the hint)

Re step 7 – most graphics formats you choose in step 3 will produce a further dialog when you perform step 6. This varies according to format type (bitmap/vector) and the format itself.

3 Click here; in the list, click a format

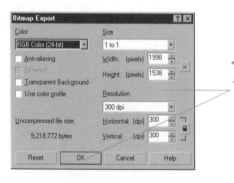

7 Complete any further dialog which launches, then click OK

Page layout

Before you can start to print out your work, you need to make sure that you've selected the correct page layout. This involves using the correct page size/orientation, and applying a style, if applicable. There are also other important issues which affect how you work with your document on screen.

Covers

Chapter Eleven

An overview

CorelDRAW gives you a lot of control over page layout. For instance, you can:

- apply a pre-defined layout style

- specify the page size you want to use

- create your own custom page size, if none of the existing sizes or layouts are suitable

- specify the page orientation

- apply a background colour

- apply a background frame

- hide the on-screen page border

- view the Printable Area

- work with facing pages (and set the start page)

- add pages at will (you can also apply non-standard sizes to new pages you insert)

- delete unwanted pages

- jump to a specific page

If you delete one or more pages in error, you can undo the deletion – see page 171.

You can set most of these before or after you create a document.

Note that you can also adjust many of these settings – in particular, layout styles – from within the Print dialog (see chapter 12). This isn't altogether a duplication, however. Instead, think of it like this. The techniques discussed in this chapter set the *drawing* parameters, while those mentioned in chapter 12 set the parameters for the *printed* output, including the paper.

CorelDRAW also provides a variety of techniques for moving around in documents. This is an important aspect of document management, especially given that CorelDRAW supports documents of up to 999 pages. You need to be able to jump instantly to the page you require.

Layout styles

CorelDRAW provides six pre-defined layout styles. These are:

- Full Page
- Book
- Booklet
- Tent Card
- Side-Fold Card
- Top-Fold Card

Imposition-ing is the process whereby pages are printed out in the order in which they need to be bound.

(For instance, in a twelve page A5 booklet, pages 1 and 12, 2 and 11 etc. might need to be printed on the same A4 sheets.)

Full Page is the default; you'll probably use this most of the time. Book and Booklet include automatic impositioning. The other layout styles are rather exotic.

Applying a layout style

1 Pull down the Layout menu and click Page Setup

2 Ensure Layout is active

3 Click here; in the list, select a layout style

You can also access layout styles within the Print dialog – see page 181.

Layout Preview

4 Click here

Setting the page size

Given the wide range of preset page sizes CorelDRAW provides, it's unlikely you'll need to define your own. However, you can do so if you need to.

To specify your own page size, follow steps 1–3. In step 4, select Custom. Now do the following in the Options dialog:

Type in a width

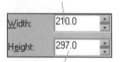

Type in a height

Finally, carry out step 5.

To match the page size to the size specified by your current printer settings, click this button:

Set From Printer

CorelDRAW comes with over forty pre-defined page sizes. It's important that you pick the right one for a given document, to ensure it prints correctly.

Specifying a page size

1 Pull down the Layout menu and click Page Setup

2 Ensure Size is active

3 Click here to produce the Page Size List

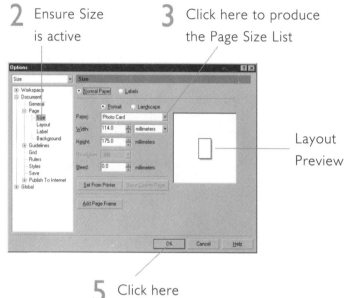

Layout Preview

5 Click here

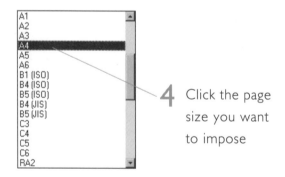

4 Click the page size you want to impose

Specifying the background colour

Orientation is an important factor in page layout. There are two kinds:

Portrait

Landscape

To specify a page orientation, follow steps 1–2 on the facing page. Now click Portrait or Landscape, as appropriate. Finally, carry out step 5.

Re step 6 – by default, the background colour can also be exported to third-party formats (see page 160). If you don't want this, deselect Print and Export Background.

You can have CorelDRAW apply any colour to the Printable Area. Once applied, the colour is – by default – printable, but you can change this if you want.

Applying a background colour

1 Pull down the Layout menu and click Page Setup

2 Ensure Background is active

3 Click here

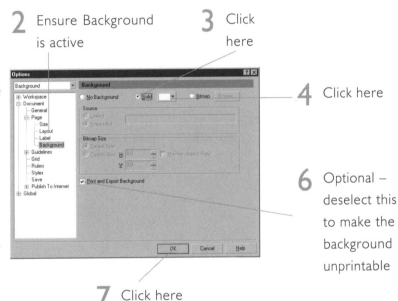

4 Click here

6 Optional – deselect this to make the background unprintable

7 Click here

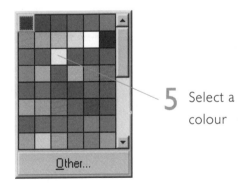

5 Select a colour

Adding a printable page frame

It's sometimes desirable to apply an outline or fill to the entire working page. You could do this manually, by defining a rectangle of the same dimensions as your current page size, superimposing it and then outlining or filling it. However, you can have CorelDRAW create the rectangle for you, automatically and much more easily – this is called adding a page frame.

Adding a page frame

1 Pull down the Layout menu and click Page Setup

2 Ensure Size is active

3 Click here

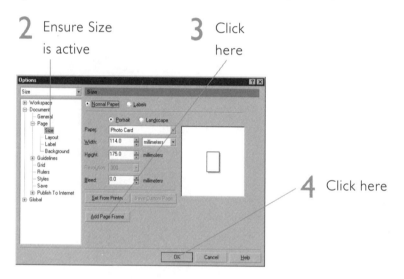

4 Click here

The Page Frame in action:

You can manipulate the page frame in the normal way. For example, you can drag it with the mouse to move it.

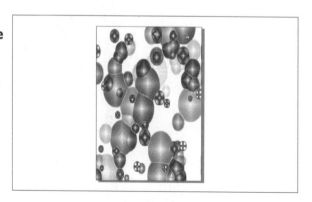

A page frame with a texture fill

Hiding the page border

By default, CorelDRAW surrounds the Printable Area with a shadowed border:

Page border

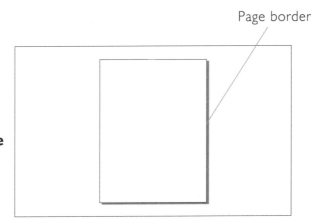

 To re-display the page border, follow steps 1–2. In step 3, select Show page border. Finally, carry out step 4.

This border serves an important function: any drawing objects which lie outside the Printable Area don't print. As a result, it's often desirable to leave the border in force.

Hiding the page border

 To view the Printable Area itself, ensure Show printable area is selected:

The dashed area is the Printable area

1 Pull down the Layout menu and click Page Setup

2 Ensure Page is active

3 Ensure this is deselected

4 Click here

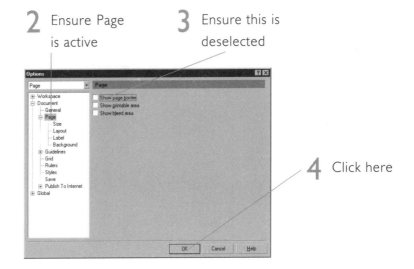

Using facing pages

CorelDRAW provides special layout options for documents with more than one page. These include:

- the ability to work with facing pages (see the illustration below)

- the ability to specify whether multi-page documents begin on a left or right page

Working with facing pages is very useful, especially (for obvious reasons) if you have graphics which span two pages, or if you need to copy or move graphics to an adjacent page. It's also useful for text work: it provides an informative overview.

Multi-page documents usually start on a right-hand page.

Look at the next illustrations:

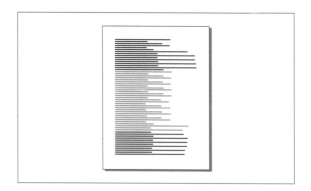

Working with single-page view

Working with facing pages

Implementing facing pages

1 Pull down the Layout menu and click Page Setup

2 Ensure Layout is active

3 Ensure this is selected

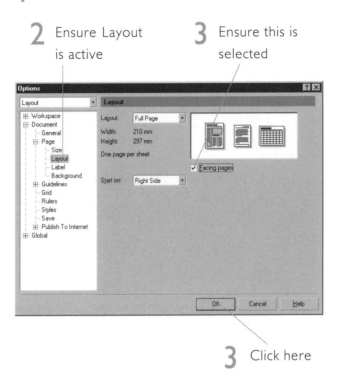

3 Click here

Caveat

Note that the Facing Pages option is not available for the following layout styles:

*   Tent cards

*   Top-Fold cards

See page 170 for how to specify start page options.

Setting the start page

When you implement the Facing Pages option for a multi-page document (see pages 168 and 169 for how to do this), you can also set an ancillary feature. You can opt to have the document begin on either of the following:

- an odd page

- an even page

Use the following as a guide. With most or all books and booklets, page 1 occurs on a right-hand page. With brochures, on the other hand, page 1 is generally an even page.

Specifying the start page

| Pull down the Layout menu and click Page Setup

2 Ensure Layout is active

3 Click here

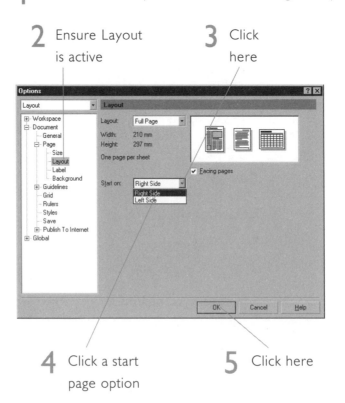

4 Click a start page option

5 Click here

Inserting pages

To delete one or more pages, pull down the Layout menu and click Delete Page.

In the Delete Page field in the Delete Page dialog, type in the number of a *single* page you want to delete. If you want to remove multiple pages, also click Through to page: and type in the number of the final page you want to delete.

Finally, in either case, click OK.

One way to convert a single-page document into a multi-page document is to add one or more new pages. This is a viable option if you want to make room for extra text or additional objects (but you don't need to do this if you're importing a text file – in this situation, CorelDRAW automatically creates as many extra pages as required).

You can specify:

• the number of pages you insert at a given time

• the reference page (the page before or after which you want the new page(s) inserted)

• whether the new page or pages are inserted before or after the reference

• the page size associated with the new pages

Adding new pages

1 Pull down the Layout menu and click Insert Page

2 Type in the number of pages you want to insert

When you delete one or more pages, CorelDRAW does not provide a warning that doing so will permanently remove the page contents.

You can, however, undo page deletions in the usual way.

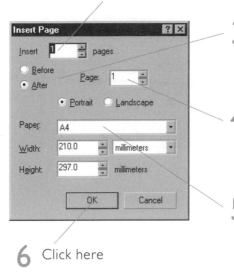

3 Select Before or After

4 Type in a reference page number

5 Optional – to give the new pages a different page size, click here and select it in the list

6 Click here

Going to specific pages

CorelDRAW provides a variety of techniques which you can use to move from one page to another. You can use:

- the Page Counter

- the Go To Page dialog

- specific keystrokes

Use whichever method most appeals, or even a combination of methods.

Using the Page Counter

See page 10 for how to use the Page Counter to jump to specific pages.

Using the Go To Page dialog

This is arguably the most convenient method for moving around in your CorelDRAW documents. However, it has one disadvantage when compared to the Counter: you have to launch the dialog as often as you need to move to another page.

 You can use a shortcut to launch the Go To Page dialog. Do the following in the Page Counter:

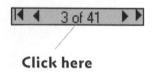

Click here

First, pull down the Layout menu and click Go To Page. Now do the following:

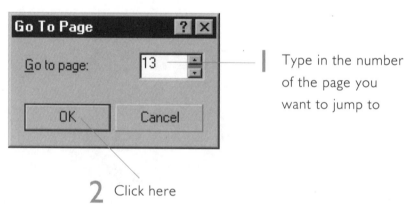

Type in the number of the page you want to jump to

2 Click here

Using keystrokes

Press Page Up or Page Down to step up or down through the available pages, one page at a time.

Printing and publishing

Most or all of your work in CorelDRAW will need to be printed, either on a desktop or higher-end printer. This chapter shows you how to tell CorelDRAW precisely what you want printed. You'll also learn how to preview your output (in a dedicated window and on-the-fly) *before* you start printing. Finally, you'll output your work to formats which can be read on the World Wide Web and use a Wizard to prepare files for service bureaus.

Covers

Chapter Twelve

Selecting your printer

Before you print your work, you should ensure CorelDRAW uses the correct printer. If you need to proof your work on a desktop printer, select this. If, however, you intend to submit your work on disk to a copy-shop or bureau, you'll need to select another (and see pages 183–185). You should also adjust your printer's setup, if applicable.

Specifying the correct printer

Pull down the File menu and click Print. Do the following:

In any incarnation of the Print dialog, you have two options when you've finished amending print settings:

- **click Print to begin printing immediately**
- **click Apply then Cancel to save your changes and close the dialog without initiating printing**

1 Ensure this tab is active

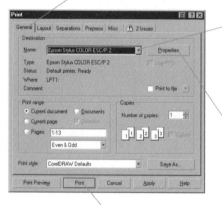

2 Click here; in the list, select a printer

3 Optional – click here and perform steps A–B below

4 Click here to begin printing (or see the HOT TIP)

Adjusting your printer's settings

Follow step 3 above to access your printer's native Properties dialog, then do the following:

This is just a sample dialog; your printer's Properties dialog may look rather different.

A Complete your printer's Properties dialog as necessary (see your manual for how to do this)

B Click here to return to the Print dialog

Selecting what to print

If you have more than one document open at once, you can elect to print multiple documents.

In the Print dialog, click Documents. Do the following:

Ensure only those documents you want to print are selected

Now carry out step 7.

CorelDRAW allows you to be very specific about what you print. You can print:

- the whole of a document
- a page range (e.g. pages 1, 3 and 6 to 10 inclusive)
- the current page
- pre-selected objects
- only odd or even pages
- specific document components (by type)

Selecting which pages to print

1 Pull down the File menu and click Print, then perform the following steps, as appropriate:

2 Click here to print all pages

3 Click here to print the current page

4 Click here to print pre-selected object(s)

5 Type in the no. of copies required

6 Enter a page range (see the HOT TIP opposite)

Re step 6 – pages are separated by commas, ranges by dashes. For example, to print pages 1, 4, 7 and 9 to 16 inclusive, enter:

1,4,7,9–16

(without a comma or stop at the end).

8 Click here to begin printing (or click Apply then Cancel)

7 Click here. In the list, choose Odd Pages or Even Pages

Printing components

An interesting and useful feature in CorelDRAW is the ability to include document components in a print run *generically*. By the same token, you can also exclude them. This is very useful for proofing your work. Component types are:

- vector graphics

- bitmapped graphics

- text

You can also specify whether CorelDRAW should print colours faithfully (you need a colour printer for this), in black or as greyscales.

Specifying print components

1 Pull down the File menu and click Print

2 Ensure this tab is active

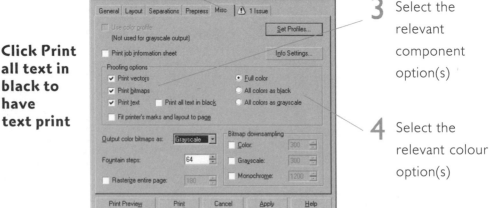

Click Print all text in black to have coloured text print in black.

3 Select the relevant component option(s)

4 Select the relevant colour option(s)

5 Click here to begin printing (or select Apply then Cancel)

Print Preview

When you launch the Print dialog (or, as here, the Print Options dialog), you have access to a useful diagnostic procedure (Preflight) which helps you iron out any printing problems.
   Click this tab:

– the textual content varies with the total of printing queries ('issues') found. Select a query at the top of the dialog; below, view details and suggested remedies.
   Click Cancel to close the dialog when you've finished, or Print if you're ready to begin printing.

After step 4, the Print Preview window launches – see page 178.

An extremely useful feature is the ability to preview your document before you initiate printing. CorelDRAW's Print Preview facility is very advanced. You can:

- (in the case of multi-page documents) preview successive pages

- print the previewed page immediately

- drag the previewed object(s) to a new location

- display coloured objects as greyscales

- have the previewed object(s) centred on the page

- have the previewed object(s) fill the page

Launching Print Preview

1 Pull down the File menu and click Print Preview, then press Ctrl+L

2 Click here to have the object(s) fill the page

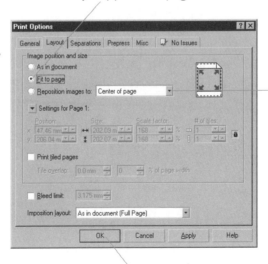

3 To centre the object(s), click here; in the list, select a centre option

4 Click here

You can use a shortcut to preview (but not amend) print jobs.

Click this button in the top right-hand corner of the Print dialog:

A miniature preview of the current page appears on the right of the dialog:

With the miniature preview window active, press Page Up or Page Down respectively to view earlier or later pages.

To close the miniaturised Preview window, re-click:

Moving previewed objects

Place the mouse pointer over the relevant object, then drag it to a new location

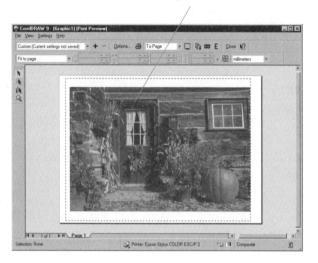

Printing the previewed page

Right-click in the Preview window; in the menu, click Print This Sheet Now

Displaying in colour

By default, coloured objects in the Print Preview window display as greyscales. To have them display in colour, do the following:

Right-click in the Preview window

2 In the menu, click Preview Color, Color

Closing Print Preview

To close the Print Preview window when you've finished using it, do the following:

Press Alt+C

Using print styles

CorelDRAW uses the concept of styles (collections of associated formatting commands) in several ways. We've already covered:

- text styles – see pages 74–75

- layout styles – see pages 163 and 181

- colour styles – see page 159

However, CorelDRAW has a further additional, and innovative feature: print styles. You can impose printing parameters and save them as a style. This means that you can apply these settings to subsequent print jobs with just a few mouse clicks.

Creating a print style

1 Make the appropriate printing adjustments (in line with the techniques discussed earlier)

2 Press Ctrl+P

3 Click this button: Save As...

4 Name the style

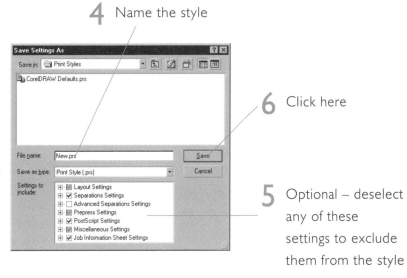

6 Click here

Re step 5: categories which have been selected have: ✔ **against them.**

5 Optional – deselect any of these settings to exclude them from the style

Applying existing print styles

│ Pull down the File menu and click Print

2 Ensure this tab is active

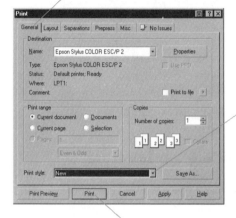

3 Click here; in
the list, select a
print style

4 Click here to begin printing (or
select Apply then Cancel)

Deleting a print style

For housekeeping reasons, it's sometimes useful to delete
an unwanted style:

│ Pull down the File menu and click Print Preview

2 In the Print Preview window, do the following:

3 Click here; in the list,
select a print style

4 Pull down the File menu and click Delete Print Style

Using layout styles when printing

 You can also apply layout styles from within the Print Options dialog (in the full-size Print Preview window) – simply follow steps 2–4.

 Layout styles which are accessible from the Print dialog are also called 'imposition layouts'.
   You have access to more layout styles in the Print dialog than in the Options dialog.

On page 163, we looked at the use of layout styles from within the relevant incarnation of the Options dialog. However, you can also apply layout styles from within the Print dialog, just before you print.

If you choose to do this, there are certain points you have to bear in mind:

- the print layout you select does not affect the document itself

- only the way you *print* the document is affected

In this way, you might have a standard CorelDRAW document set up – via the Options dialog – as Full Page (the default). However, if you wanted to print out a proof copy (as multiple thumbnail images on one sheet), you might select any of the Print dialog layout styles which relate to this e.g: 3 x 3(9up) or 4 x 3(12up).

Applying a layout style before printing

1 Pull down the File menu and click Print

2 Make sure this tab is active

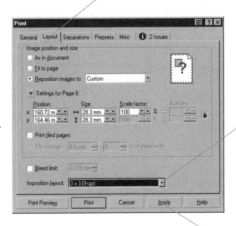

3 Click here; in the list which launches, click a layout style

 Re step 4 – click Print instead if you're ready to begin printing.

4 Click here, then Cancel

Proofing aids

Re step 3 – to apply a new registration mark, do the following:

Click here; select a mark in the list

Re step 5 – the colour bar is a row of the six fundamental colours (red, green, cyan, blue, magenta and yellow) – use this to verify the fidelity of printed output.

To print page numbers and/or crop marks, select Print page numbers and Crop/fold marks respectively.

Re step 6 – click Print instead if you're ready to begin printing.

You can have CorelDRAW append a variety of additional material to your printed output. This is a valuable technique for proofing your work.

The most frequently used examples are:

- file information – i.e. the name, date, time and filename (if applicable) at the foot of each sheet

- page numbers

- crop marks (an aid in aligning/trimming your output)

- registration marks (an aid in aligning colour separations)

- a colour calibration bar across each sheet (see the DON'T FORGET tip for how to use this)

Using proofing aids

1 Pull down the File menu and click Print

2 Ensure this tab is active

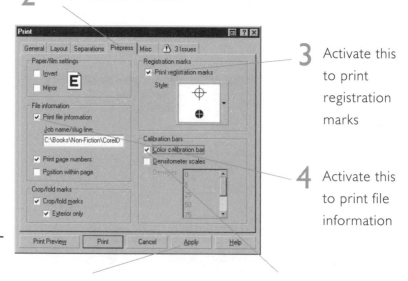

3 Activate this to print registration marks

4 Activate this to print file information

6 Click here, then Cancel

5 Activate this to print a colour bar

Printing to a file

Consult the copy-shop or bureau – before you print your work to file – to avoid snags.

You can have CorelDRAW print a file to disk rather than directly to your printer. This may be useful if you intend to have your work printed by a copy shop or service bureau. You simply take the disk to them and they should be able to output the document more or less automatically.

When you choose to have CorelDRAW print a file to disk, it produces a PostScript file with the extension .PRN. This should be usable by any bureau.

Re step 3 – if your print file will be used on an Apple Mac computer (frequently the case with bureaus), click:

In the menu, click For Mac. (Select Pages to Single Files if you want a separate .PRN file for each page – this also applies to PC files.)
Now carry out steps 4–8, as appropriate.

Perform step 6 as often as necessary, until you reach the correct folder.

1 Pull down the File menu and click Print

2 Ensure this tab is active

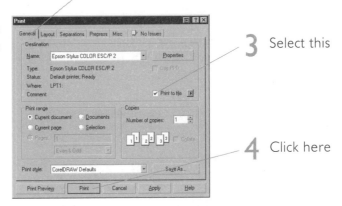

3 Select this

4 Click here

5 Click here. In the drop-down list, click the drive you want to host the print file

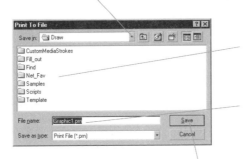

6 Double-click the folder to which you want to save the file

7 Name the print file

8 Click here

The Bureau Wizard

The bureau may be able to edit .PRN files (via programs such as Adobe Distiller).

We saw on page 183 how to create a .PRN file for transmission to a copy-shop or service bureau. However, this has disadvantages, chief of which is that it's possible the bureau will not be able to verify/correct the .PRN file.

There are other options, though. You can send your work:

1. as a .CDR file (though not all copy-shops or bureaus welcome these)

Use the Prepare For Service Bureau Wizard to make sure you don't omit any information which is vital to your service bureau.

2. as a PostScript file

Although you can use the techniques discussed on page 160 manually to export your work as an .EPS file, the best method to use for both 1. and 2. above is the Prepare For Service Bureau Wizard.

Running the Prepare For Service Bureau Wizard

Pull down the File menu and click Prepare For Service Bureau. Do the following:

Re step 1 – select one of the following options:

- **Choose a profile provided by your service bureau – if your bureau has supplied a profile, this is often the best option**
- **Gather all files associated with this document – CorelDRAW collates the necessary files to enable accurate printing**

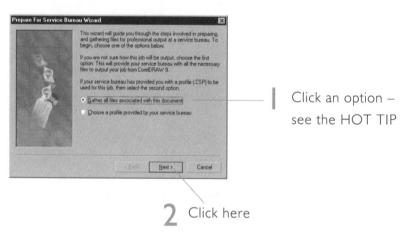

Click an option – see the HOT TIP

2 Click here

3 If, in step 1, you selected Choose a profile provided by your service bureau, ignore steps 5–9. Instead, select the profile in the next dialog, then follow the on-screen instructions

4 If, in step 1, you selected Gather all files associated with this document, perform steps 5–9

...cont'd

PDF (Adobe Acrobat) files are designed to preserve typefaces, graphics and formatting in a format which can be read by users who do not have the originating program, on just about any platform. (PDF files are often downloaded to the Internet or intranets.)

The Prepare For Service Bureau Wizard produces various file types (e.g. PostScript and CorelDRAW), as appropriate.

If you adopt the method listed in step 3, you'll need to download Corel's Service Bureau Profiler, from: www.corel.com

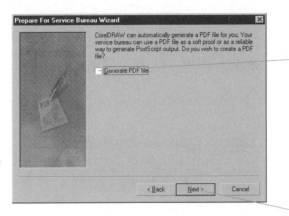

5 Click here if you want a PDF file produced – see the DON'T FORGET tip

6 Click here

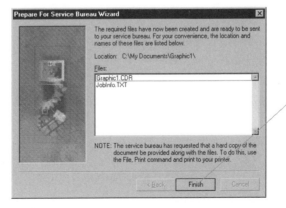

7 Type in details of where you want the files stored

8 Click here

9 Click here

Publishing to the Internet

HTML (Hypertext Mark-up Language) Language) is the standard Internet file format. In CorelDRAW, it's designed to reproduce image content faithfully.

You can publish your work in HTML format, for use on the Internet.

Publishing to the Web

I Pull down the File menu and click Publish to Internet

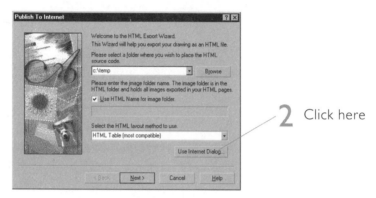

2 Click here

To create an extra HTML file listing document information e.g:

ensure Statistics Page is selected. (The list displays on the left of your browser.)

3 Click here; in the list, select an HTML layout

4 Type in details of the destination folder

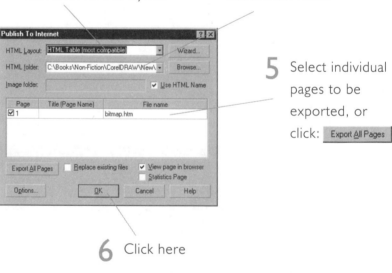

5 Select individual pages to be exported, or click: Export All Pages

After step 7, send the resultant files to the Internet, using whatever method you normally employ.

6 Click here

7 The exported HTML file is opened in your browser. When you've finished proofing it, press Alt+F4

Index

P